Journal of Legal Technology Risk Management

Volume 1	Spring 2007	Issue 1

Current Issues In the Field of Legal Technology Risk Management

© 2006 by Journal of Legal Technology Risk Management -- ISSN 1932-5584 (Print)

Journal of Legal Technology Risk Management

VOLUME 1 — Spring 2007 — ISSUE 1

Current Issues In the Field of Legal Technology Risk Management

2006 – 2007 Board of Editors

Editor-in-Chief
Daniel B. Garrie, Esq. (U.S.A.)

Managing Editor
Dr. Giuseppina (Pina) D'Agostina (Canada)

Executive Editor
Matthew Armstrong (U.S.A)
Dr. Sylvia Mercado Kierkegaard (Denmark)

Scientific Council
Director Stephanie A. "Tess" Blair (U.S.A.)
Honorable Amir Ali Majid (U.K.)
Honorable Justice Jumpol Pinyosinwat (Thailand)
Professor Geraint Howells (U.K.)
Professor Andres Guadamuz (U.K.)
Professor Carlos Rohrmann, Esq (Brazil)
Honorable Justice Ivor Archie (Trinidad & Tobago)
Professor Emeritus Gary T. Marx (U.S.A)
Mr. Bill Burdett (U.S.A)
Managing Partner Eric A. Capriloi (France)
Professor Donald P. Harris (U.S.A)
Kelly Merkel, Esq (U.S.A)
Dr. Larry Ponemon (U.S.A)
Mr. Carlo Cardilli (U.S.A)
Dr. Thomas J. Routt (U.S.A)

Members
Matthew Armstrong, JD (U.S.A.;, Attorney)
Janet Coppins (U.S.A.; Patent Examiner at USPTO)
Eleni Kosta, LLM (Belgium; Legal Analyst)
Paolo Balboni, JD (Netherlands; Attorney in Italy)
Salvatore Scibetta, Esq. (U.S.A., Attorney)
Ygal Saadoun (France, Legal Media Risk Analyst)
Steve Williams (U.S.A., Media Risk Analyst)
Rebecca Wong, LLB,MSc,LLM,PCHE (United Kingdom, Professor)

About the Journal of Legal Technology Risk Management

The *Journal of Legal Technology Risk Management* (ISSN 1932-5584) is published twice per year by top legal professionals and scholars from the law, technology, and business industries. The views expressed in the *Journal of Legal Technology Risk Management Policy* are those of the authors and not necessarily of the *Journal of Legal Technology Risk Management* or the Lexeprint Inc -- the publishing company.

Form: Citations conform to *The Bluebook: A Uniform System of Citation* (18th ed. 2005). Please cite the *Journal of Legal Technology Risk Management* as 1 J.L. & Tech. Risk Management __ (2006).

Copyright: All articles copyright © 2006 by the *Journal of Legal Technology Risk Management* except where otherwise expressly indicated. For all articles to which it holds copyright, the *Journal of Legal Technology Risk Management* permits copies to be made for classroom use, provided that (1) the author and the *Journal of Legal Technology Risk Management* are identified, (2) the proper notice of copyright is affixed to each copy, (3) each copy is distributed at or below cost, and (4) the *Journal of Legal Technology Risk Management* is notified of the use.

For reprint permission for purposes other than classroom use, please submit request as specified at daniel@ltrm.org

Manuscripts: The *Journal of Legal Technology Risk Management* seeks to publish articles making original contributions in the field of public policy. The *Journal* accepts both articles and compelling essays for publication that are related to the expansive topics of technology, law, and business risk management. Manuscripts must contain an abstract describing the article or essay which will be edited and used for publication on the website and in CD-ROM format. The *Journal* welcomes submissions from legal scholars, technologists, mathematicians, analysts, academics, policy makers, practitioners, lawyers, judges and social scientists.

Electronic submissions are encouraged. Submissions by email and attachment should be directed to submissions@ltrm.org.

Subscriptions: Subscription requests should be e-mailed to daniel@ltrm.org

Internet Address: The *Journal of Legal Technology Risk Management* website is located at http://www.ltrm.org

Journal of Legal Technology Risk Management

VOLUME 1	Spring 2007	ISSUE 1

HOW TO STUMP A CORPORATE LAWYER: MEANS OF EFFECTIVE LEGAL RISK MANAGEMENT FOR IP COUNSEL   1
Kelly Merkel, Esq.

DISABILITY PER SE IS NOT BAR TO JURY SERVICE   8
Dr. Amir A. Majid

CORPORATE GOVERNANCE IN AN EMERGING MARKET: A PERSPECTIVE ON PAKISTAN   22
Haroon H. Hamid, JD
Valeria Kozhich, JD

RECONSIDERING REGULATION: A HISTORICAL VIEW OF THE LEGALITY OF INTERNET POKER AND DISCUSSION OF THE INTERNET GAMBLING BAN OF 2006   34
Christopher Grohman

NETWORK SECURITY ABSTRACT   75
Julie Machal-Fulks

HOW TO STUMP A CORPORATE LAWYER: MEANS OF EFFECTIVE LEGAL RISK MANAGEMENT FOR IP COUNSEL

Kelly Merkel, Esq.[1]

I) INTRODUCTION

A recent headline announced that GCs are most concerned about compliance matters within their companies, and that this worry even surpasses concern about outside counsel costs. Although the implementation and complexity of Sarbanes-Oxley and related laws often bear the blame for GCs' concerns, compliance at all levels of corporate operations is increasingly problematic.[2] It is therefore no surprise that GCs are working more closely with in-house intellectual property (IP) counsel (or drawing from the GCs' own IP experience) to demand higher accountability for a company's IP holdings.[3]

For multinational corporations, the IP portfolio is now well recognized as an asset with licensing and litigation potential, as well as a liability with the potential for indemnity claims and the potential for allegations of corruption (most likely via defense on inequitable conduct and fraud). GCs require and demand increased multidisciplinary knowledge from IP counsel as shareholders and regulatory bodies identify more risks at every level of corporate operation. IP counsel should not lose sight of the primary role as caregiver of the client's IP portfolio, even upon the assumption of increasing responsibility in multidisciplinary roles on behalf of the corporate client.[4] In these roles, however, a comprehensive and successful legal risk

---

[1] Ms. Merkel is Assistant General Counsel, Intellectual Property for American Standard's global Bath & Kitchen business. Ms. Merkel has notable experience in drafting, prosecution ad management of complex patent and trademark applications and notable experience in the area of management of domain name portfolios, including filing and prosecution of domain name disputes. Prior to working for American Standard she worked for Ladas & Parry in New York and Hoffmann & Baron in New Jersey.

Ms. Merkel is also an active member of the American Intellectual Property Law Association working on the Asian Patent Practice Committee. In addition, Ms. Merkel has written and spoken on patent law in the context of the USPTO. Ms. Merkel is admitted to the USPTO, Court of Appeals for the Federal Circuit, and the State and District Courts of New Jersey.

[2] Martin C. Daks, "Compliance, Not Legal Fees, Named as GCs' Chief Concern" (November 1, 2006), New Jersey Law Journal, http://www.law.com/jsp/article.jsp?id=1162375513514 ("a new study released October 23...shows that 86 percent of 169 companies surveyed in 2005 say their main concern is 'keeping track of company activities that might have legal implications.")

[3] The author adopts the following definition of "IP" from Stanley P. Kowalski and R. David Kryder, "Golden Rice: A Case Study in Intellectual property Management and International Capacity Building", 13 Risk: Health, Safety and Environment 47 (Spring 2002)("IP is taken to mean, without limitation, IP rights, including patent rights, plant variety protection certificates, unpublished patent applications, and any inventions, improvements, an/or discoveries that may or may not be legally protectable including know-how, trade secrets, research plans and priorities, research results and related reports, statistical models, computer programs, related reports, market interests and product ideas.")

[4] Henry W. Jones III, "Other Software Licensing Pitfalls (Beyond Black-Letter Law Errors): Common Erroneous, Risky Assumptions of Clients & Counsel", *Understanding the Intellectual Property License*, 879 PLI/Pat 157 (2006)(The author emphasizes that tasks traditionally not within the province of the legal department have become increasingly important to effect proper compliance in the reigning regulatory environment. Activities such software management are "not just IT's turf. Finance, legal and other internal and external corporate constituencies will need to know if, how and why the business is partly based on "non-

1

management program requires integration of the IP counsel's province as existing and effective means of reducing exposure at all levels of IP procurement, excision and exploitation.

Thus, IP counsel's particular attention to the preparation of opinions and drafting of underlying IP contributes highly to the success of the company's risk management efforts. These tasks, taken in combination with non-traditional forums of indemnity and cyberlaw, help IP counsel focus on the greatest risks inherent in the company's IP operations and relieve GCs of at least one item from an ever-increasing regulatory agenda.

II) OPINIONS ARE LIKE EMERGENCY FUNDS: EVERYBODY SHOULD HAVE ONE

For in-house IP counsel, the most evident form of risk management technique is the preparation of legal opinions that allow IP counsel to assess the client's position.[5] This begins with a determination of what the client already owns or controls and the identification of IP that is clearly in the public domain or can be reasonably acquired.[6] The opinion is generally based on a series of questions that typically foster further questions into not only the validity of the IP and the claim to ownership but also the treatment of the IP in the client's tax and regulatory structures.[7] IP counsel, during preparation of the opinion, should therefore use the opportunity for Q&A to elicit further answers concerning marketing strategies (including any potential trademark clearances that may be required, advertising claims that may be subject to scrutiny by regulatory agencies and competitors, site of manufacture, terms of employment and dealings with foreign regulatory authorities).[8]

---

traditional IP such as open-source software (OSS). The author states, "Future Sarbanes-Oxley reviews may include [these] concerns. Plan ahead for, and begin now, internal, iterative education, standards, setting, confidentiality, audit, policy, vendor discussions and renegotiations and other interactions outside the typical past years' MIS sphere.")

[5] Stanley P. Kowalski and R. David Kryder, "Golden Rice: A Case Study in Intellectual property Management and International Capacity Building", 13 Risk: Health, Safety and Environment 47 (Spring 2002) ("IP rights risk management...begins with a systematic product clearance (PC)....Producing a timely, proactive PC is a wise resource expenditure... It permits an early assessment of the IP landscape and allows management decisions to be made well in advance regarding which components, technologies and processes are best to incorporate into the product under development in order to avoid using those which are not owned or cannot be readily licensed . . . and thus, is a risk management opinion regarding a particular product at a particular time for a particular country.")

[6] Warren D. Woessner, "Preparing Patent Legal Opinions", 876 PLI/Pat 77, 86 (2006)(citing M.R. Dzwonczyk et al., "Strategies for Effective Opinion Drafting", *AIPLA Advanced Biotechnology/Chemical Patent Practice Seminar – 2002 Roadshow*, (2002)). From a patent perspective, a true assessment of the company's full portfolio includes ascertaining whether there are live patents, expired patents and proprietary technology that comprises one or more trade secrets. IP counsel should always identify, and in an acquisition, also acquire, all patents that have expired within the last six years so as to hold the right to sue for past infringement of such patents.

[7] Kowalski and Kryder. These questions elicit information such as the methods and procedures that went (or will go) into producing a product; the product's principal components; the essential ingredients that constitute each principal component; the rights that may be attached to each component and its ingredients; who seems to own such rights; and the client's position in the industry that prompted development of the product.

[8] John Goff, "Coming Distractions: If These Eight Risks are not on Your Radar Screen They Will be Soon", CFO Magazine (April 1, 2006). The fact gathering for an IP opinion is an excellent opportunity to discuss any meetings that your business leadership will have with members of another organization or with

Included in the analysis is a review of whether all proper assignments have been effected and an ultimate determination of ownership has been made (i.e., consultation of ownership records, fee payment records, files corresponding to pending applications and an explanation of how each patent relates to the company's products or services). This critical step, being both ethical and legal, often uncovers any information that can affect the validity of the company's claim to IP rights and may very well affect the valuation of any patent or other IP that is in the company's possession or is being considered for licensing or acquisition (and thereby exposing the company to potential indemnity and regulatory claims). Such information may have nothing to do with the treatment of the IP right during drafting and everything to do with treatment of the IP right post-issuance.[9] This type of review, and the legal opinions derived therefrom, should therefore extend to the company's entire IP portfolio.[10]

It is noted that failure to provide an opinion may be in legal compliance with the company's litigation strategy and prevailing state and federal rules governing the business operation.[11] The disciplinary rules of the states in which IP counsel and the GCs are licensed, however, may require that such an opinion be rendered as part of the attorneys' duties of fiduciary duty and agency.[12]

III) GETTING THE BEST DRAFT PICK

Another well-recognized risk management tool for IP counsel is the cautious and effective drafting of the IP portfolio, particularly in representation before national offices. During litigation, hindsight scrutiny of the drafting attorney's conduct often raises skepticism regarding the extent to which the attorney exhibited ethical behavior. For instance, failure to investigate the merits of a patent infringement case prior to filing suit, and failure to reasonably inquire about facts material to patentability, is only two of the many reasons cited in declaring a

---

representatives from the local government (for instance, to ensure compliance with the United States Federal Corrupt Practices Act, which exacts strict penalties for giving or taking bribes overseas). Such reconnaissance will require cooperation with colleagues in other practice areas to ensure effective execution of an overall legal risk management program.

[9] Consider the situation wherein a potential licensor offers the client company an exclusive license to a family of patents. Independent review of the target portfolio reveals that the subject patents had been placed in receivership after a lengthy investigation of the licensor by the SEC. The potential licensor therefore had no rights to transfer to the client. In this situation, counsel's due diligence mitigated the risk that the company would not only have worthless IP in its portfolio but also excised any potential claims made on behalf of the receiver and the SEC against the company.

[10] *See* Claude Brodesser, "Warner Ponies Up 'Hazzard' Pay", (June 29, 2005), www.variety.com). In June 2005, Warner Bros. agreed to pay a Georgia-based movie producer at least $17.5 million for infringing on the producer's copyright of a little-known movie entitled "Moonrunners". The 1974 film formed the basis of the popular television show "The Dukes of Hazzard". In 1978, Warner Bros. attained the rights to "Moonrunners" to make the TV series; however, the movie rights remained with the producer of the original movie. At the time of the lawsuit, Warner had already spent $53 million making the movie and $40 million on the marketing budget. The threat of a permanent injunction prompted Warner Bros. to quickly settle or face indeterminate delay of the movie premiere as well as preemption of DVD sales.)

[11] FN 5: *see* Knorr – Bremse Systeme Fuer Nutzfahrzeuge GmbH v. Dana Corp., 383 F.3d 1337 (Fed. Cir. 2004)(The Federal Circuit ruled that no adverse inference shall be drawn from the failure to obtain an opinion of counsel or the failure to disclose the opinion of counsel in a patent infringement case.

[12] Such rules are typically considered to be consistent with practice-specific rules (such as those promulgated by the USPTO governing the conduct of its registered attorneys and agents in demanding more than mere compliance).

finding of inequitable conduct.[13] Such a finding transforms the potential returns from an infringement action from an asset into a liability that can run afoul of the client's indemnity provisions. A finding of inequitable conduct can therefore open the door for suits by the client against the practitioner for breach of fiduciary duty and malpractice, even years after prosecution has ended.[14]

Principles of inequitable conduct and fraud are not limited to patents but also apply to other areas of intellectual property practice.[15] In fully educating the business regarding IP valuation and reliance on a properly administered IP portfolio, IP counsel must tread carefully also with respect to the role of drafting in brand valuation (as such valuation often affects shareholder value and is highly scrutinized in any acquisition or divesture of a relevant business unit or during any tax, customs or other regulatory audit).[16] IP counsel for multinational companies must consider, in their risk management strategies, the actions of aggressive local tax authorities which may not only target sales within the country boundaries but also factor potential sales targeted via traditional and electronic marketing means.[17] IP counsel must also ensure that all statements made in the registration of valuable trade marks and trade names (and corresponding domain name registrations) accurately reflect the actual current designation of goods by the mark.[18] This requires an appreciation of the brand beyond source identification

---

[13] *See* View Eng'g Inc. v. Robotic Vision Sys., 208 F.3d 981 (Fed. Cir. 2000)("In bringing a claim of infringement, the patent holder, if challenged, must be prepared to demonstrate to both the court and the alleged infringer exactly why it believed before filing the claim that it had a reasonable chance of proving infringement." (208 F.3d at 986); see also Braessler USA, LLP v. Stryker Sales Corp., 267 F.3d 1370 (Fed. Cir. 2001)("Attorneys must conduct meaningful inquiries when the surrounding circumstances would cause a reasonable attorney to understand that relevant and questionable material information should be assessed."(267 F.3d at 1385)).

[14] David Hricik, "Where the Bodies Are: Current Exemplars of Inequitable Conduct and How to Avoid Them", 12 Tex. Intell. Prop. L.J. 267 (Winter 2004)(citing Lex Tex Ltd. V. Skillman, 579 A. 2d 244, 16 USPQ 2d (BNA) 1137 (D.C. 1990)(in 1985, Federal Circuit declared patents issued in 1963 to Lex Tex to be unenforceable, resulting in reversal of $9 million judgment in favor of Lex Tex against infringer; Lex Tex subsequently sued the patent attorneys for failing to disclose pertinent prior art to the USPTO during patent prosecution 20+ years earlier).

[15] *See* Ready Productions, Inc. v. Cantrell, 85 F. Supp. 2d 672, 691 (S.D. Tex. 2000)("Under copyright law, 'the knowing failure to advise the Copyright Office of [material] facts . . . Constitutes grounds for holding the registration invalid and incapable of supporting an infringement action."). It is further imperative for IP counsel to obtain a list of the client's registered copyrights along with a list of unregistered copyrights that are material to the business. Counsel must identify the creators of material copyrightable works to ensure that the client owns the work (this includes obtaining copies of all licenses, security interests, payment obligations, and lists of all third party intellectual property).

[16] Since trademark rights are inherently associated with brand value, some insurers have developed formulae for covering damage to the brand.

[17] IP counsel should coordinate with members of the client's IT and communications teams to obtain a list of domain names that the client owns and has registered. This information is most efficiently administered by an established corporate domain name service such as Iron Mountain.

[18] *See* Linda K. McLeod, "Knew or Should Have Known, Reckless Disregard for the Truth and Fraud Before the Trademark Office", AIPLA Quarterly Journal, Volume 34, Number 3, p. 287, 299 (Summer 2006)("...recent decisions identify the elements of fraud as: (1) a false representation or withholding of information; (2) regarding a material fact; and (3) the person making the presentation or withholding the information knew or should have known that it was false or misleading."); see also *Standard Knitting Ltd. v. Toyota Kabushiki Kaisha*, 77 USPQ 2d (BNA) 1917, 1932 (TTAB 2006)(The first citable decision issued by the Unites States Trademark Trial Appeals Board provides that any corporate officer, in executing a declaration of trademark use, states that all goods cited in the description of goods are actually in use at the time the

when drafting the description of goods, taking licensing opportunities and consequent global brand expansion into full consideration.[19]

IV) MASTERING THE CYBER DOMAIN

IP counsel's execution of an effective risk management strategy will fail without proper dedication of resources to the client's cyber activities. The client, through its officers, employees, agents and vendors is generating an electronic identity. Yet the client may be simultaneously participating in various forms of "identity theft" via the appropriation of information from a plethora of online sources.[20]

Clients have long underestimated the capability of officers, employees, agents and vendors to inadvertently compromise proprietary information via electronic means (for instance, via personal email transmissions, sharing of hyperlinks or blog discussions). It therefore becomes IP counsel's responsibility to mitigate the risk of compromise to the greatest extent possible via contractual indemnity clauses and the policies to back them up.[21] The allocation of risk among the client and a plurality of licensees, vendors and employees comprises an alternate and complex means of risk management that is used to valuate existing IP (whether properly licensed or not) and/or create new IP (i.e., created for the client for its own or others' use, created by combining existing IP with proprietary information and potentially adding new subject matter). Education of all of these parties therefore becomes essential for them to understand where the risks lie and what behavior (perhaps legal, but not ethical) enhances the likelihood of loss under the current relationship.[22]

---

declaration is made, that the officer personally knows such statement is true and, if the officer does not know, (s)he is obligated to investigate thoroughly before signing and filing the declaration.)

[19] Because trademarks exist for the benefit of the consumer, increasingly there is recognition that product defects should be attributed to the party that owns the source identifier even if that party is not the manufacturer. *See* Conrad Weinman, "Trademark Licensors and Product Liability Claims – A European Perspective", *95 Trademark Rep. 1394*, (November-December 2005)("[T]the trademark licensor is primarily threatened by product liability claims based on domestic laws passed recently by national governments to implement [the EC Directive on Product Liability], which included among the persons deemed to be the "producer of a product " any person who, by "putting his name, trademark or other distinguishing feature on the product presents himself as the producer".)

[20] *See* The IQ Group, Ltd. v. Wiesner, 409 Supp. 2d 587 (D.N.J. 2006)(Plaintiff The IQ Group prepared email advertisements that included an IQ logo as well as a hyperlink which, when clicked, directed the user to a page on IQ's website that allegedly contained copyright notices. Defendants distributed the same ads and removed the IQ logo and hyperlink. Since the logo was the identifying symbol and the hyperlink led to identifying information about the copyright holder, IQ alleged that removal of these items violated section 1202 of the Digital Millennium Copyright Act (which bars the alteration or removal of copyright management information ("CMI"). The court rules that a construction that allows a logo, which functions as a service mark, to be treated as CMI would essentially turn trademark claims into DMCA claims, creating "a species of mutant trademark/copyright law, blurring the boundaries between the law of trademarks and that of copyright law". The court declined to blur such boundary.

[21] Henry W. Jones III at 162 ("Counsel shouldn't assume that software maintenance/support is 'standard' and doesn't need process definition, robust definitions, risk management and clear balance of obligations on both sides...").

[22] *See* Lisa M. Brownlee, "Part III. Valuation: Chapter 12A. Insurance Coverage Considerations", *IP Due Diligence in Corp. Transactions*, Sec. 12A:1 (June 2006)("The size of a company's relevant insurance portfolio will vary depending on the size of the company, the scope of its operations and the vision of its risk management department...Even if liability exposure for possible intellectual property and business tort

Cyber-risk insurance policies and third party coverage for cyber liability vary widely. Although many include personal injury coverage for libel, defamation and invasion of privacy, some cyber forms also cover negligent acts, which lead to the transmission of information to another computer by the insured which causes damage; breaches of security; and loss resulting from an insured's hosting activities or its conduct of e-commerce. Several types of third-party cyber policies also provide some coverage for intellectual property liability such as copyright, patent, service mark, trademark and trade secret infringement. The policies also cover various types of unauthorized access to a computer system (including, without limitation, data theft/loss, plagiarism, loss or theft of electronic information, commercial appropriations and unfair competition). IP counsel should expect clients' use of e-commerce insurance to increase significantly to supplement conventional loss control strategies such as firewalls, virus software and the vigilance of network technicians.[23]

IP counsel should ensure that technological measures of protection have been deployed to control prolific unlicensed copying, or that valid business reasons exist for free distribution.[24] This includes implementing policy and business rules that mandate strict adherence to license terms and conditions for copyrightable works such as free open-source software (FOSS) (wherein it is advisable to retain qualified legal counsel to advise about FOSS licensing and use automated tools to track licenses and changes). IP counsel must work closely with outside counsel and the GCs to fully understand the consequences combining FOSS and proprietary software and evaluate the strength of any indemnities. Development of a contingency plan is a vital element (basically risk management of the risk management plan) that will allow the client to continue operating even if infringing code is taken out of production.[25]

V) "IT IS NOT ENOUGH TO DO YOUR BEST – YOU MUST DO WHAT IS REQUIRED."

GCs and IP counsel therefore must appreciate that effective execution of intellectual property management, as part of comprehensive risk management plan, can generate additional

---

claims against it...policies in existence at the first date that damages could be asserted in an intellectual property lawsuit must be considered in connection with the analysis of how coverage for such claims may expand or diminish value of the company's assets.")

[23] Robert Paul Norman, "Starting and Managing an Online Business: Chapter 2. Using E-Commerce Insurance to Minimize Liability", *1 Internet Law and Practice*, Sec. 2:37. Norman asserts that businesses that do not carry such coverage do so at a great risk in view of the value of computer and internet assets. Newer policies cover several types of internet and network risks through internet media liability coverage; internet professional services liability coverage; security liability coverage; cyber-extortion coverage; information asset coverage; business interruption coverage; and crisis management coverage (this latter policy covers risks such as failure to protect confidential information, violations of private information and the failure to prevent transmission of a virus. According to Norman, this kind of policy is a real asset as part of a comprehensive risk management program directed at Internet losses.

[24] Lisa M. Brownlee, "Intellectual Property Due Diligence in Corporate Transactions: Part II. Intellectual Property Audits: Chapter 8. Copyright Audit", *IP Due Diligence in Corp. Transactions*, Sec. 8:68 (June 2006)).

[25] *Id.* ("Ideally....[a] Company will have established mechanisms for tracking the source code – whether open source or proprietary-used in its products and/or services. However, absent such systematic record-keeping, the task of identifying open source software issues, in particular, will be a particular challenge for due diligence team members.")(citing Federal Deposit Insurance Corporation, "Risk Management of Free and Open-Source Software", http://www.fdic.gov/news/financial/2004/FIL11404a.html (last visited March 1, 2006).

revenue for companies and thereby increase shareholder value. IP counsel needs to work with GCs and clients to execute an offensive risk management strategy that includes analyzing emerging standards and competitor focus in order to acquire a competitive advantage.[26] In the specific situation involving the acquisition or divestiture of a business, IP counsel should view transfer of the IP portfolio as an exhibition of multiple concurrent financial behaviors. IP counsel should also use this opportunity to coordinate with other corporate counsel as part of an overall legal risk management plan that preserves the maximum value of the IP portfolio during the transfer yet complies with all applicable regulatory provisions (i.e., Sarbanes-Oxley).[27]

The inherent volatility in intellectual asset value itself therefore comprises a risk to the business that may not be captured on the balance sheet.[28] Although comprehensive legal risk management strategies will comprise a variety of multidisciplinary issues, the inherent exposure in the IP portfolio warrants a realistic analysis concerning the level of compliance the client is willing to achieve and the extent of risk the client can legally assume.

---

[26] Dennis Fernandez and Laurie de Leon, "Exploitation of Emerging Technological Applications in Biosecurity", 30 October 2006, http://legal-journal.com ("This approach entails the consideration of an effective business plan alignment, adequate research of competitor technology, partner IP rights positioning and/or acquisition, enforcement models, business methods and platform development. Ownership of a core technology is on the first step into an emerging market; success is largely determined by the management of a strong IP portfolio since IP supports future revenue streams, erects barriers to competition and imprints a company's perceived value to investors, partners and acquirers.")

[27] Nir Kossovsky, M.D., Robert J. Block and James M. Singer, "Intellectual Asset M&A Due Diligence and Risk Management", 6 NO 11 *Pat. Strategy & Mgmt.* 6 (2006)("[I]ntellectual assets by their nature tend to generate volatile returns if the owner does not fully appreciate and manage associated risks.").

[28] *Id.* Volatility in intellectual assets is generally present in three forms. First, there is first party risk, wherein the IP owner loses a legal right to asset returns (i.e., estoppel). Second, there is third party risk, wherein the IP owner must indemnify third parties in connection with a dispute over asset rights, or wherein the IP owner is identified as the alleged infringer of stronger claims to an intellectual asset (i.e., the IP owner incorporates third-party code in proprietary software). Third, there is transfer risk, wherein the IP owner incurs liability in connection with the transfer of intellectual property (i.e., the internal transfer pricing understates asset value and consequently incurs tax penalties).

DISABILITY PER SE IS NOT BAR TO JURY SERVICE

Dr. Amir A. Majid[1]

I. INTRODUCTION

Regarding civil rights of disabled people, I have not come across any test of welfare more potent than that authoritatively enunciated in the UK House of Lords by Lord Slynn of Hadley (a jurist of brilliant distinction). Lord Slynn adopts a purposive and justice-oriented approach to this issue and recommends that a nation should strive to enable a disabled person lead as "normal life" as possible. His Lordship emphasized that "the yardstick of a "normal life" is important; it is a better approach than adopting the test as to whether something is 'essential' or 'desirable'. Social life in the sense of mixing with others, taking part in activities with others, undertaking recreation and cultural activities can be part of normal life. It is not in any way unreasonable that the severely disabled person should wish to be involved in them despite his disability."[2]

It is a well-known fact that jury is "representative of the community as a whole."[3] Therefore, the disabled members of "the community", over 8 million in the UK, cannot be left out of this role fairly. This precept comes into a sharp relief and becomes pivotally applicable when the accused of a crime or civil wrong is disabled himself/herself.

---

[1] Honorable Majid has published a law book and 35 articles in British, German, Dutch and American learned journals, as well as 50 journalistic items. Honorable Majid was the first blind person in the world to be a barrister and DCL (Dr. of Civil Law). Honorable Majid holds a BA (Punjab), LLB Hons-LLM (London) DASL, Dip in Air & Spc Law (London Institute of World Affairs), DASL-Dr. of Civil Law (McGill), FRSA, Barrister (Lincoln's Inn), and is a member of the Higher Education Academy. Dr. Majid is also a reader in International Law, London Metropolitan University; Practising Barrister; part-time Immigration Judge Adjunct Professor in Law, Webster University of USA ; External Examiner of the Boards of Examiners: University College London, Cert. n Air & Space Law University of London, Dip. in Air & Space Law University of London, LLM University of London, Dip. in Int'l Law.

Furthermore, Honorable Majid was an erasmus Lecturer, 2003, Frankfurt, Germany; 4 times Guest Lecturer at the National Defence college, Islamabad; 3 times Guest Lecturer at the Institute of Strategic Studies, Islamabad; 2 times Guest Lecturer, Pak Institute of International Affairs, Karachi. Dr. Majid has published a law book and 35 articles in British, German, Dutch and American learned journals, as well as 50 journalistic items.

[2] Cockburn v. Chief Adjudication Officer, 1 W.L.R. 799 (1997), 3 All ER 844-870 (H.L 1997) (also known as Halliday); see Prof. Nick Wikeley, Cases: Benefits, Bodily Functions and Living with Disability, 61 M.L.R. 551, 556 (1998) (referring to the Department's attempt to confine the need for attention to "essential", as opposed to "desirable" communication, said that it "seems at best outdated and at worst grossly insensitive to the position of those with hearing loss"; see also Amir A. Majid, Anachronistic Judicial Approaches to Disability Benefits Law, 15 Denning L.J. 93-112 (2000) (exploring this concept in more detail).

[3] See, e.g., Taylor LCJ in Richard Dimbleby lecture 1992 where he said, "In every criminal trial the jury decides the facts and the need for the decision to be representative of the standards of society as a whole is satisfied by the verdict being that of 12 jurors selected at random." ("The Judiciary in the Nineties" by Lord Taylor of Gosforth - The Richard Dimbleby Lecture (also known as the Dimblebly Lecture) was founded in the memory of Richard Dimbleby, The famous BBC broadcaster. It has been delivered by an influential business or political figure almost every year since 1972 (with gaps in 1981, 1991 and 1993) at http://en.wikipedia.org/wiki/Richard_Dimbleby_Lecture); see also Douglas Silas, Have You Heard? The Jury is Out!, Legal Action, Dec. 1999, at 6.

On 9 November 1999 a Crown Court judge in Woolwich, London, rejected a request of a profoundly deaf person, Mr. Jeff McWhinney, who wanted to serve on a jury and wished to participate in the administration of justice and did not want to benefit from the discharge of summons releasing him from the jury service. Mr. McWhinney was called to serve on a jury but when the court discovered that he was profoundly deaf, the summons were discharged. Mr. McWhinney had achieved the distinction of being the first Chief Executive of the British Deaf Association (BDA) at the age of 39 and the judge had praised him as "an intelligent, hard working, responsible man who has made a great contribution to life."[4]

The judge refused to reinstate the summons. The Disability Discrimination Act (DDA) 1995 calls upon service providers, including courts and tribunals to make reasonable adjustments so as not to discriminate disabled persons by treating them less favorably for a reason relating to their disability. Judge Anwyl held that the "jury service" did not fall within the ambit of the Act; it was not a "service to the public."[5]

More disappointingly the judge held that Mr. McWhinney could perform with the aid of a signer but it would mean that the jury room will have the thirteenth person and that would amount to an "incurable irregularity." Thus the deaf people remained excluded from this great service in the UK.

S. 9B, as inserted by the Criminal justice and Public Order Act 1994 (UK), in the JURIES ACT 1974 provides:-

1. Where it appears to the appropriate officer, in the case of a person attending in pursuance of a summons under this Act, that on account of physical disability there is doubt as to his capacity to act effectively as a juror, the person may be brought before the judge.
2. The judge shall determine whether or not the person should act as a juror; but he shall affirm the summons unless he is of the opinion that the person will not, on account of his disability, be capable of acting effectively as a juror. In which case he shall discharge the summons.
3. In this section "the judge" means any judge of the High Court or any Circuit judge or Recorder.

The issue was adjudicated upon earlier in *In re* Osman[6], by Sir Lawrence Verney, Recorder of London. Sir Lawrence said that the presence of a deaf juror is "likely to leave the Defendant with the fear that juror while perhaps helped to understand what is being said must inevitably have lost any nuances available to his colleagues from the manner and tone of voice in which answers are given. Where assessment of the credibility of a witness is important, as so often it is, that juror may not be capable of acting as effectively as the others.

This reason was not accepted as a valid one by the judge in the McWhinney case. About this, she said, "I am satisfied ... and I do not see that there are practical hurdles to being a sign interpreter assisting a juror in court." Recognising that the 1994 Act, by S.9B, had created a

---

[4] R v. A Juror, (Nov. 9, 1999) (unreported transcript, on file in Woolwich County Court, London, England) (all quotes from the judge and submissions hereafter are from the Transcript); Also Clare Dyer, Legal Correspondent, Deaf Chief Executive Ruled Out as Juror, The Guardian, Nov. 10, 1999.

[5] Jon Robins, Falling on Deaf Ears, Law Society Gazette, Feb. 3, 2000; Amir A. Majid, The UK Disability Discrimination Act - Definitional Maze and Enforcement Barriers 36 Braille Forum 8, 33-38 (1998) (new changes in law, like the DDA 2005, hope to improve the situation in this regard).

[6] *In re* Osman, 1 W.L.R. 1327 (C. Crim. Ct. 1995).

presumption in favor of a disabled person to serve on a jury, the judge emphasized that the Disability Discrimination Act 1995 makes positive provisions for providing communication help to an individual. Where a Claimant, Defendant, witness or any other person is required to attend a court, the sign language interpreters are allowed to assist them. This is now mandatory under Part III of the Disability Discrimination Act 1995, except where it can be evidenced that such provision is not "reasonably" possible.

Judge Shirley Anwyl heard in the case that 7 States in the US accepted deaf jurors and the experience of the New York Supreme Court showed that the deaf jury members had served "with distinction." She further observed that "It is quite plain from the experience of the American courts, where the deaf jurors have been allowed to sit on juries and be aided by a 13th person in the jury room, that far from being a hindrance, it has been felt in many cases to be of assistance." The US courts have found in some cases that the inclusion of a deaf juror had brought a special and valuable perspective to the process.

Regrettably the judge found the second reason sufficient to justify her negative decision. *In re* Osman Sir Lawrence, believing that he was bound by CA precedents, had given his second reason thus: "It has long been held that it is an incurable irregularity for an independent person to retire with the jury even though he may take no part in the discussion. An interpreter would be bound to take a part even though not expressing any personal opinion."

The court had the help of an amicus curiae in the McWhinney case who was, this author has to observe most regrettably, not attuned with the modern attitudes towards disabled persons. The same amicus, Mr. Dennison, helped the Old Baily in the Osman case in 1995. As he had persuaded Sir Lawrence Verney to reach wrong decision, he made it difficult for a relatively progressive judge in the McWhinney case to make a proactive decision in favour of disabled people. He submitted to Judge Anwyl QC:

> "As the law in this country stands, there is a bar on the thirteenth person of any description accompanying the jury in their retirement. Unfortunately for Mr. McWhinney, I say this and I mean this, in his case he could not sit and serve on the jury without that facility. There are people who could cope, and have coped, on their own in a jury retirement room. But a person who cannot cope without that assistance, in the light of the law as it stands, must be found to be not capable of acting effectively as a juror."

Mr. Dennison had not improved his knowledge about the progressive development in this field. As he had done so in 1996 in the Osman case, he supported his above submissions in both cases by two appeal cases.[7] This author finds two elements in the preceding submission of Mr. Dennison reflecting poorly on the role of an "amicus curiae" as follows:

The force he unfairly gave to his submission to maintain this unsatisfactory state of affairs against disabled jurors by saying that in no " the thirteenth person of any description" was allowed in the jury room; corollary of it being the exclusion of a sign language interpreter He fails to inform the court that in the Goby case an officer of the court was involved and any reference to "any person" was not part of the ratio decidendi of the case.[8] Secondly, and more

---

[7] Goby v. Wetherill, [1915] 2 K.B. 674; R. v. McNeil, 1967 Crim. L.R. 540 (C.A.)

[8] Goby v. Wetherill, [1915] 2 K.B. 674 (In fact, in this case in the Ramsgate County Court in a trial the jury retired to consider their verdict in charge of an official, called the town Sergeant, who acted as the usher of the Court. The town Sergeant went into the retiring room with the jury and remained there for about twenty minutes while they were considering their verdict).

importantly, The enunciations in the Goby case had to be viewed in the light of the fact that it was decided in 1915, 3 years before for the first time the women over 30 were given right to vote by Representation of People Act 1918.

The tone of his submission and the use of phrases like "I say it and I mean it" and "must be found to be not capable of acting effectively as a juror " indicated as if he were fighting a cause against disable people. With respect, the amicus could have indicated that some discretion was left to the judge for making a progressive decision and perhaps encourage a new approach signaled by the presumption in favour of disabled jurors introduced by the 1994 Act. It is note worthy that the 1994 legislation was dealing with " Criminal Justice and Public Order" but had given special attention to improve the civil rights of disabled people by inserting this presumption by S. 41 in the Juries Act 1974.

When The Lord Chancellor's Department (now Department of Constitutional Affairs) was asked to advise on the issue, it had replied there was no binding precedent or legislative provision forbidding the assistance of a sign language interpreter as a thirteenth person to a deaf juror.[9] If nothing else, this fact should have inspired the amicus curiae to submit fairly that so far "the 13th stranger" had not expressly found by any binding precedent to include a "sign language interpreter" helping a deaf person acting effectively as a juror. Further, he could have found support in the submission of Mr. McWhinney's counsel, Paul Taylor, when he said:-

> "As the case of Guzman suggests the principles referred to in McNeil and Goby relate to strangers who have nothing whatsoever to do with the deliberations, do not facilitate them and are simply officers of the court. That is very different to someone who is there to actively facilitate those discussions and who is simply seen as an ajunct to the juror whose rights it is to participate at that stage."

The judge ignored the pro-disabled submissions and attached definitive weight to Mr. Dennison's submissions and refused to reinstate the jury summons of Mr. McWhinney. She stated, "But unless and until the Parliament changes the law, I, like any other Circuit Judge, am bound by the decision of the Court of Appeal and I cannot allow a stranger in the jury room."

It is most respectfully submitted that the judge had before her sufficient material to reject the second reason as well. There was, as it is edumbrated above, no legal provision dictating the interpretation that the expression "stranger" in the jury room included "a sign language interpreter."

II. PROGRESSIVE TREATMENT OF HARD OF HEARING PEOPLE IN THE US

The deaf people are treated very well in America, even though the hard of hearing activists, understandably, wish the authorities to do more in this field. The alert survey of that country reveals that the UK state of affairs is manifestly untenable.

---

[9] Douglas Silas, Juries - Deaf Jurors, 143 New L.J. 896 (June 18, 1993).

Under Title II of the Americans with Disabilities Act[10], every state and local court is prohibited from discrimination based on disability. The U.S. Department of Justice has issued regulations explaining the requirements of that Act.[11]

All American courts are required to provide auxiliary aids and services by the ADA. The Judicial Conference of the Administrative Office of the United States Courts has adopted a policy that all federal courts will "provide reasonable accommodations to persons with communications disabilities."[12] This obligation is translated into the provision of sign language interpreters or other appropriate auxiliary aid to deaf and hard of hearing participants in court proceedings, at the expense of the judiciary, in accordance with guidelines prepared by the Administrative Office of the United States Courts.[13]

The ADA and the regulations made thereunder apply to the local and state courts and they are required to provide auxiliary aids to ensure effective communication with deaf and hard of hearing individuals in civil, as well as criminal proceedings. Their obligations can be summarized[14] as follows:

- A public entity shall take appropriate steps to ensure that communications with applicants, participants, and members of the public with disabilities are as effective as communications with others. [15]
- A public entity shall furnish appropriate auxiliary aids and services where necessary to afford an individual with a disability an equal opportunity to participate in, and enjoy the benefits of, a service, program, or activity conducted by a public entity. [16]
- In determining what type of auxiliary aid and service is necessary, a public entity shall give primary consideration to the requests of the individual with disabilities. [17]

Deaf and hard-of-hearing persons have a right to communicate effectively and to participate in proceedings and activities conducted by all state and local authorities. Under this right, specifically, they are entitled to have courts provide and pay for auxiliary aids to enable them to understand and be understood. The ADA protects all persons participating in court activities, including litigants, witnesses, jurors, spectators and attorneys. It applies to any type of court proceeding in any type of state or local court, including civil, criminal, traffic, small claims, domestic relations, juvenile and other specialized courts. It also applies to other activities conducted by court systems, such as personnel, educational activities, and communications with clerks and other court personnel.

For deaf persons who use sign language, the most effective auxiliary aid which a court can provide is usually the service of qualified sign language interpreters, trained in legal procedure and terminology. For deaf persons who do not use sign language and who have good levels of reading comprehension, the appropriate auxiliary aid is usually the use of a computer-

---

[10] 42 U.S.C. §§ 12131-12134 (1990).

[11] 28 C.F.R. § 35 (2006) (U.S. Department of Justice Final Rule: Non discrimination on the Basis of Disability in State and Local Government Services).

[12] Judicial Conference of the United States-Sept. 1995, p. 40 at http://www.uscourts.gov/judconf.html.

[13] The guidelines are published in Vol. I, Administrative Manual, Chapter III, General Management and Administration, Guide to Judiciary Policies and Procedures. at http://www.uscourts.gov/judconf.html

[14] 28 C.F.R. § 35.160 (2006).

[15] 28 C.F.R. § 35.160 (2006).

[16] 28 C.F.R. § 35.160 (2006).

[17] 28 C.F.R. § 35.160 (2006).

assisted transcript, or CAT, system. Through this system, a court reporter enters the words spoken during the proceeding into a computer, which simultaneously transcribes the words onto a computer screen which can be read by the deaf person. For other persons, an oral interpreter may be needed to facilitate lip reading.

For those who benefit from hearing aids, the appropriate auxiliary aid would be amplified or modified sound equipment, a courtroom with appropriate acoustic properties, and/or assistive listening systems. However, the appropriate auxiliary aid depends on the amount of hearing, the communication skills and the literacy skills of the individual. Court officers should confer with the deaf or hard of hearing individual to determine the appropriate services or modifications for effective communication for that individual.[18]

Although "primary consideration" is to be given to the request of the disabled person (a mature recognition of the individuality of a disabled person) the parents of a minor who is the subject of a juvenile proceedings, or any other carers, are clearly "participants" in the proceedings even though the parents or carers are not formal parties; they may not be even witnesses but they are entitled to qualified interpreting services during the proceedings.

To prevent the confining of the meanings of "aids" to hardware, the U.S. Department of Justice regulation defines the term "auxiliary aids" for deaf and hard of hearing individuals to include qualified interpreters and computer-aided transcription services.[19] In its Analysis of the regulation, the Department of Justice uses the computer-aided transcription system as an example of an effective auxiliary aid or service in a courtroom for a person who is deaf or has a hearing loss who uses speech to communicate.[20]

The ADA regulation has also made it clear that the individual with a disability cannot be charged for the auxiliary aid provided by a state or local court; it says:

> "A public entity may not place a surcharge on a particular individual with a disability . . . to cover the costs of measures, such as the provision of auxiliary aids or program accessibility, that are required to provide that individual . . . with the nondiscriminatory treatment required by the Act."[21]

Some state courts still have laws that permit state judges to assess the cost of interpreter services as "court costs." The Department of Justice has already recognized that imposition of the cost of courtroom interpreter services is impermissible under section 504 of the Rehabilitation Act of 1973.[22] Accordingly, recouping the costs of interpreter services by assessing them as part of court costs would also be prohibited.

---

[18] For instance, it should be borne in mind that the American Sign Language (ASL), as opposed to Signed English, is a language completely distinct from English, and is the native language of most deaf American. Signed English is a rendering of ASL signs into English word order and grammar. A deaf person who uses ASL will not always be able to communicate fully or successfully in written or Signed English. Many interpreters are competent only in Signed English.

[19] 28 C.F.R. § 35.130(f) (2006).

[20] Nondiscrimination Based on Handicap In Federally Assisted Programs—Implementation of Section 504 of the Rehabilitation Act of 1973 and Executive Order 11914, 45 Fed. Reg. 37,620, app. 37,630 (June 3, 1980).

[21] 29 U.S.C. § 794 (2002).

[22] 28 C.F.R. § 42.504 (2006).

Section 504 of the Rehabilitation Act of 1973 provides, "no otherwise qualified handicapped individual in the United States . . . shall, solely by reason of his handicap, be excluded from participation in, be denied the benefits of, or be subjected to discrimination under any program or activity receiving Federal financial assistance."[23]

Since the promulgation of Section 504 of the Rehabilitation Act in 1973 almost all of the US police departments (indubitably receiving financial assistance from one or more federal agencies) have been subject to giving equal treatment to deaf or hard of hearing persons. Even if an interpreter is not required, police officers should take other steps to ensure effective communication, such as writing information and making other accommodations in their usual practices. The Department of Justice (DOJ) Regulation states that the bodies covered by the 1973 Act, employing fifteen or more persons, "shall provide appropriate auxiliary aids to qualified handicapped persons with impaired sensory, manual or speaking skills where a refusal to make such provision would discriminatorily impair or exclude the participation of such persons in a program receiving Federal financial assistance."[24] Such auxiliary aids may include . . . qualified interpreters . . . . Department officials may require recipients employing fewer than fifteen persons to provide auxiliary aids when this would not significantly impair the ability of the recipient to provide its benefits or services.[25]

The National Association of the Deaf[26] Records the analysis of the Department of Justice of this Regulation as it relates to law enforcement agencies as follows:

> "Law enforcement agencies should provide for the availability of qualified interpreters (certified where possible, by a recognized certification agency) to assist the agencies when dealing with hearing-impaired persons. Where the hearing-impaired person uses American Sign Language for communication, the term "qualified interpreter" would mean an interpreter skilled in communicating in American Sign Language. It is the responsibility of the law enforcement agency to determine whether the hearing-impaired person uses American Sign Language1 or Signed English to communicate. If a hearing-impaired person is arrested, the arresting officer's Miranda warning should be communicated to the arrestee on a printed form approved for such use by the law enforcement agency where there is no qualified interpreter immediately available and communication is otherwise inadequate. The form should also advise the arrestee that the law enforcement agency has an obligation under Federal law to offer an interpreter to the arrestee without cost and that the agency will defer interrogation pending the appearance of an interpreter."[27]

The Analysis of the DOJ specifically places the responsibility on the recipient agency to ascertain the type of sign language with which the deaf individual feels most comfortable, and then to secure an interpreter who is competent in that language. Questioning of deaf persons

---

[23] 28 C.F.R. § 42.503(f). (2006).
[24] National Association of the Deaf, *Police and Law Enforcement Agencies*, at http://www.nad.org/policelawenforcement. (The author is grateful to the contributors on this website).
[25] Id.
[26] Id.
[27] Id.

should also take place only with an interpreter present in order to comply with Section 504 and to achieve reliable communication.[28]

The obligations of the law enforcement agency to deaf or hard of hearing persons who have been arrested or held for questioning are safeguarded by ordinary US Constitutional and statutory law. The American courts have excluded evidence obtained from a deaf defendant where it was found that the Miranda warning (dealing with the Constitutional Rights of an individual) was not adequately communicated to the defendant.[29] In these cases, the warnings were conveyed in sign language, but were not broken down to the defendant's language level. Securing of an interpreter with an RID Legal Skills Certificate for a timely interpretation of the rights, accompanied with careful explanation and breakdown of every legal term and sign, is one way a law enforcement agency may prevent objections to the adequacy of this communication, as well as comply with the legal requirements of Section 504. Presentation of a printed Advice of Rights form without an interpreter will seldom, if, be sufficient.

The police officers have been advised not to utter Miranda warnings to deaf people if a lawyer is not present; and videotaping both the Miranda warning and their waiver has also been suggested.[30]

Many law enforcement agencies videotape all communications with deaf defendants in order to be able to substantiate the effectiveness of the communication and the quality of the interpretation. All deaf persons must be informed of the law enforcement agency's obligation to have a free, qualified interpreter present during all communications. This can usually be achieved, as the Analysis suggests, by use of a printed card before the arrival of the interpreter. However, the agency must be aware of the fact that some deaf persons have very limited English language skills, and will require an interpreter to ensure comprehension of even this message.

As of 26 January 1992, under the ADA and its regulations, local and state law enforcement agencies are required to provide qualified sign language interpreters, and other auxiliary aids, to ensure effective communication with deaf and hard of hearing individuals.[31] Deference must be given to the deaf or hard of hearing individual's choice of what auxiliary aid he or she needs.[32]

The Analysis to the Title II regulation to the ADA specifies where an interpreter may be needed. It states:

"Although in some circumstances a notepad and written materials may be sufficient to permit effective communication, in other circumstances they may not be sufficient. For

---

[28] *Id.*

[29] State of Maryland v. Barker, Crim. Nos. 17,995, 19,518 (Md. Cir. Ct. Dec. 8, 1977); State of Oregon v. Mason, Crim. No. C 80-03-30821 (Or. Cir. Ct. May 27, 1980). Currently the typical Miranda warning is, "You have the right to remain silent. Anything you say can and will be used against you in a court of law. You have the right to speak to an attorney, and to have an attorney present during any questioning. If you cannot afford a lawyer, one will be provided for you at government expense." The Supreme Court had overturned a conviction due to the omission of this kind of warning (exact words are not essential) in Miranda v. Arizona, 384 U.S. 436 (1966). The Supreme Court once again confirmed it later in Dickerson v. United States, 530 U.S. 428 (2000).

[30] McCay Vernon et al., *Deaf Murderers: Clinical and Forensic Issues*, 17 Behavioral Sciences and the Law, 495-516 (1999).

[31] 28 C.F.R. § 35.160 (2006).

[32] 28 C.F.R. § 35.160(b)(2) (2006).

example, a qualified interpreter may be necessary when the information being communicated is complex, or is exchanged for a lengthy period of time. Generally, factors to be considered in determining whether an interpreter is required include the context in which the communication is taking place, the number of people involved, and the importance of the communication."[33]

People who are deaf or hard of hearing have the right to do business, to engage in the national economy, and have the same opportunities for economic empowerment and independence as anyone else. Title III of the Americans with Disabilities Act (ADA) protects these rights. In June 2006 National Association of Deaf (NAD) forced Morgan Stanley (a finance house) to settle in such a way that now the American deaf and hard of hearing people will not be prevented from transacting stocks and securities by using Telecommunications Relay Services (TRS); now these services are acknowledged by the Morgan Stanley to be a "secured option."[34]

In this agreement, Morgan Stanley has agreed to accept trade orders placed through a relay service by clients who are deaf or hard of hearing, when such trade orders would be accepted if placed by telephone. Morgan Stanley has also agreed to provide notice and training to internal personnel responsible for accepting trades via telephone.[35]

Section 504, the ADA, and the Title II regulation also require public entities which provide emergency telephone service to be accessible to deaf callers. "Telephone emergency services, including 911 services, shall provide direct access to individuals who use [TTYs] and computer modems."[36]

The Analysis to this regulation clarifies that the term "direct access" means that "[t]elephone emergency access through a third party or through a relay service would not satisfy the requirement for direct access."[37] The Analysis goes on to explain:

The requirement for direct access disallows the use of a separate seven-digit number 911 service is available. Separate seven-digit emergency call numbers would be unfamiliar to many individuals and also more burdensome to use. A standard emergency 911 number

---

[33] 56 Fed. Reg. 35,694, 35,712 (July 26, 1992).

[34] National Association of the Deaf, NAD Lawsuit Against Morgan Stanley Settled, (June 14, 2006), at http://www.nad.org/site/pp.asp?c=foINKQMBF&b=1776833.

[35] Id. (Relay services enable individuals who are deaf or hard of hearing, as well as individuals with speech impairments, to engage in communication in a manner that is functionally equivalent to the ability of a telephone user. Relay services are available in all 50 states, the District of Columbia, Puerto Rico, and the U.S. territories for local and/or long distance calls. Relay service providers are compensated from either a state or a federal fund; there is no cost to the user. A relay service call may be initiated by anyone, with or without a hearing or speech disability. Relay services are now available for many modes of accessing telecommunications, including text-to-voice (using a TTY, also known as a telecommunications device for the deaf, or TDD), voice/hearing carry over, Internet Protocol relay, video relay, captioned telephones, and other forms of relay services as so defined under Title IV of the ADA by the Federal Communications Commission).

[36] 28 C.F.R. § 35.162 (2006).

[37] 56 Fed.Reg. 35,694, 35712 (July 26, 1991) (U.S. Department of Justice Final Rule: Nondiscrimination on the Basis of Disability in State and Local Government Services).

is easier to remember and would save valuable time spent in searching in telephone books for a local seven-digit emergency number.[38]

The Section 504 Regulations also explicitly require the installation of telecommunication devices for deaf and hard of hearing persons in offices having telephone contact with the public, such as police departments. Deaf individuals should be able to make both incoming and outgoing calls to police agencies, if hearing persons are permitted to make such calls. The United States Department of Justice Section 504 Regulations require recipients to provide auxiliary aids such as telephone devices to deaf and hard of hearing persons.[39] In the Analysis of these Regulations, the Department of Justice notes that:

> Law enforcement agencies are also required to install TTYs or equivalent mechanisms . . . to enable persons with hearing and speaking impairments to communicate effectively with such agencies.[40] Where a TTY is required under the ADA, there is a corresponding requirement that it should be maintained in operable working condition.[41]

III. CAN THE UK LEARN FROM THE US?

In Mr. McWhinney's case, discussed in the first part of this article, the judge was informed about the sensible approach taken in the US to the matter of deaf jurors in the cases of *Guzman* and *Dempsey*.[42] In *Dempsey* the American federal court was specifically concerned with the presence of the "additional person" in the jury room. Finding that the presence of an interpreter was not a ground for a new trial, The Tenth Circuit District Court had ruled that "the presence of the interpreter in the jury deliberation room was not a problem for jury confidentiality, and had no inhibiting or other influence on the jury."

In the other case Judge Bud Goodman had robustly stated, "Like members of any other cognizable group, the deaf are a part of our community and must be considered, evaluated, and finally either accepted or rejected for service as individuals just as any other citizen. The grounds for exempting the deaf from jury service have vanished. People who are otherwise qualified cannot be challenged from cause under New York statutory law or the Constitution of this state or of the United States, solely on the basis of deafness."[43]

The Code of Ethics of Interpreters requires "neutrality, confidentiality and true and faithful interpretation. The interpreter also takes the judicial oath at the beginning of the proceedings. He/she can be clearly reminded of the terms of S. 8 of the Contempt of Court Act 1981. This section states that it will be a contempt of court to disclose "any particulars of statements made, opinions expressed, arguments advanced or votes cast by members of the jury in the course of deliberations."

---

[38] 56 Fed. Reg. 35,713 (July 26, 1991).
[39] 28 C.F.R. § 42.503(f) (2006).
[40] Nondiscrimination Based on Handicap In Federally Assisted Programs—Implementation of Section 504 of the Rehabilitation Act of 1973 and Executive Order 11914, 45 Fed. Reg. 37,620, app. 37,630 (June 3, 1980).
[41] 28 C.F.R. § 35.133 (2006).
[42] People v. Guzman, 478 N.Y.S.2d 455 (N.Y. Sup. Ct.1984); United States v. Dempsey, 830 F.2d 1084 (10th Cir. 1987).
[43] *Guzman*, 478 N.Y.S.2d at 467.

In the hearing of 9 November 1999 of the McWhinney case, technical information about "variation of vocal cords", "inflection of voice" and "observance of voice related-demeanour" was presented to the court. The judge was impressed by this scientific data and said that she saw no legal or practical impediment for a deaf person to perform a juror's role. Disabled people would find this an offensive route to determine their "civil right" - how many ordinary jurors are subjected to these tests?

Having made the preceding point, this author would most respectfully submit that a general non-technical test of "capacity to effectively act as a juror" should be sufficient to allow a deaf person to join a jury. In fact, many judges would agree with him that "demeanour" "confident speech", "smiles" and "dress" are more often used as tools of deception by cunning witnesses. In many judicial training courses, the author had the fortune of attending, learned speakers, backing their statements with cogent statistical evidence, have been at pains to caution against exaggerated dependence on "the medium" of delivery of evidence, and have strongly advised the judges to focus on "the substance."

Barrister Enright boldly states, "In the final analysis, the notion that decisions about honesty cannot be determined by the deaf or the blind may be nothing more than the arrogance of the able-bodied."[44] Realistically observing some problems which may arise in rare cases, he says, "difficulties are avoided by discussion between lawyers and the list office - where there is a will there is a way."

As a part-time Immigration Judge, since appointment in November 1997, this author has dealt with over 1200 cases and his blindness has not surfaced as an impediment in a single case. Further, his performance has not been worse than his sighted colleagues because he could not "see" the demeanour of witnesses appearing before him.[45] The biased judicial noises lose their cover when, a court with no disabled person involved in its staff or jury, is not able to evaluate the lexical nuances of the testimony of a foreign witness which are supposed to be so all important to ascertain his/her credibility.

In the McWhinney case the judge was sympathetic to the problem of deaf jurors and commented "I am interested, and indeed pleased to understand that the Lord Chancellor is actively considering the question of changing the law so that there can be assistance given to a deaf juror." In a Disability Law Conference on 13 February 1999, the Lord Chancellor, Lord Irvine, had acknowledge that "the current prohibition of any juror requiring assistance of a carer in a jury room" was one of "the concerns to be addressed in considering access to the law for disabled people."

Another distinguished deaf person, directly affected by this judgement, Mr James Strachan (chief executive of the Royal National Institute for Deaf People, UK) said, "The ruling demonstrates the need for a fundamental review of this outdated law. I find it ridiculous that I can be a chief executive, sit on a government task force and run a multi-million pound business but am unable to serve on a jury."[46]

---

[44] Sean Enright, *The Deaf Juror and the Thirteenth Man*, 149 New L.J. 1720, (Nov. 19, 1999).
[45] He may look a flash Harry but he has to make this point. In the first 3 years of his judicial function it was stated that 43% decisions of the Immigration Judges were appealed to higher courts and although appealing in the immigration field in many cases is no more than a device to prolong the Appellant's stay in the UK his personal performance indicated an appeal rate of 29%.
[46] *A Deaf Person's Verdict*, The Guardian, Nov. 11, 1999.

The disabled people are only interested in fair recognition of their capabilities and wish to obviate the insult that that they are incapable of performing on a jury effectively. Like many other people they may prefer to avoid the service which, to some, brings them face-to-face with criminals. According to the UK Home Office research published on 10 November 1999, for instance, two-thirds of people summoned to serve on juries managed to get out of it. The research found, "Only a third of 50,000 called up for jury service over a six week period ... were available, and half of those succeeding in having their service deferred, pleading work, holiday or urgent commitments."[47] Many profoundly deaf persons in the UK would not be able and/or willing to act as a juror and what is submitted is the evaluation of an individual person whether he/she will be able to perform satisfactorily.

Mr Greg Heller, a distinguished American deaf person, was invited to give the inaugural speech to the 1996 graduating class by the Missouri School for the Deaf. He highlighted the point that, "My purpose in life was to educate him that deaf people can do it." He related a personal story about being called for jury duty a few years ago. The court clerk told Heller's interpreter that he would not be able to serve on the jury because of his hearing impairment. Rather than give up on serving on a jury, Heller chose to educate the clerk about the abilities of deaf people."[48]

In the aftermath of the McWhinney case there were other public expressions of sympathy. Mr. Tom Clarke, MP, raised the issue in the House of Commons. The British Prime Minister, Mr. Blair, replied, "It should be possible for all people to take part in jury service. Of course it is a very great public service and people do engage in jury service and we should do everything to encourage them." He further said, "The Home Secretary informs me that we are reviewing the rules on that matter because it should be possible for all people to take part in jury service." Mr. McWhinney welcomed this support and said that "[t]he ban on deaf jurors is an affront to the deaf community and undermines the credibility of the justice system."[49]

The Department for Constitutional Affairs Website (as of 10 January 2007) contains the evidence of inertia on this topic. Commenting about the issue the Royal National Institute for Deaf People (RNID), the largest charity representing the needs of the 8.7 million deaf and hard of hearing adults in the UK, pleads with the British government thus, "Our main concern is around the issue of deaf jurors. RNID is disappointed that the review does not appear to address the problems of deaf people undertaking jury service."[50]

When "deafness" had " vanished" as a ground of challenged in the US in 1984, and the presence of the extra person as a sign language interpreter failed to persuade the US federal court to overturn a verdict in 1987, the judge in the McWhinney case had the ability to distinguish between "a stranger" and a court-authorized interpreter, subject to some strict controls, facilitating a deaf juror's work.

---

[47] Clare Dyer, Legal Correspondent, *Two in Three Manage to Get Off Jury Service*, The Guardian, Nov. 11, 1999.
[48] Central Institute for the Deaf Alumni Association, *CIDAA Bulletin*, (1996), at http://www.cidaa.org/CIDAA%20Bulletins/Fall96/Autumn_1996_Bulletin.html
[49] A Land Mark Case in the British Legal System, British Deaf News, Dec. 1999, at 1.
[50] Department for Constitutional Affairs Website, *The Criminal Courts Review Report: Comments Received from Human Rights/Civil Liberties Organisations* -3, at http://www.dca.gov.uk/criminal/auldcom/hr/hr3.htm (last updated July 3, 2006).

The Royal Association for Deaf people (RAD), illustrating its point by referring to some serious cases including the April 2000 trial of John Paul Works in Kentucky (where the accused faced death penalty for the shooting of Regina Nickles, the first female police officer in Kentucky to be killed in the line of duty), said that deaf people were serving on jury in the US without any problem, why not in the UK. Commenting on the anachronistic situation in the UK, the RAD said, "State courts are required to ensure that people who are deaf or hard of hearing have an equal opportunity to benefit from the courts' programs and services, including participation as jurors, parties, witnesses and spectators. So if a system like this can work successfully in the USA, why can a similar system not be implemented in the UK?"[51]

Concluding on this controversy, this author has to observe with profound disappointment that, what could have been corrected by Judge Anwyl by imaginative legal reasoning, remains unaltered as of February 2007 by politicians. No wonder disabled people view immaculate expressions of reforms in the normative and material provision in the disability field with cynicism.

IV. WHAT IS THE FUTURE?

Whilst in an article a terrible picture of detrimental discrimination against disabled lawyers has been recorded, some heartening changes in the British attitudes have been observed as well. Miss Nihar Punj, a profoundly deaf person since birth, received a Law Society diversity scholarship last year and finished her Legal Practice Course (LPC) at BPP Law School, London. Scheduled to join a City firm, the 23-year-old has had a commendable positive experience in finding a training contract. She is taking up a training contract with an eminent firm of solicitors, Herbert Smith, starting in September 2007. She said, "Most firms were very open about my hearing impairment and did not view it as an obstacle." Based on her experience, refreshingly she says, "I do feel that the legal profession is gradually becoming more enlightened about disability issues. The fact that Herbert Smith has offered me a training contract demonstrates that City firms are accepting of disabilities as long as you have drive and determination to succeed."[52]

The Law Society ran a campaign to give deaf people a fair chance of legally-aided representation. Consequently, from October 2005 the deaf clients will now have reasonable costs of a British Sign Language interpreter met by the Legal Services Commission, even when the deaf persons are seeking legal advice.[53]

The author was invited in a conference on disability equality issues on 12 April 2006 held in London. The British Minister for Disabled People, Ms Anne McGuire, participated in it. When the author drew her attention to his article "Jury still out on deaf jurors", she promised to look into the matter afresh. Indeed, she has obtained a copy of the article from the author and is currently reviewing the matter.[54]

---

[51] Royal Association of Deaf People, *Deaf People are Serving on Juries in the USA, So Why Not Here?*, The News, (Mar. 21, 2000), at http://www.royaldeaf.org.uk.

[52] Grania Langdon-Down, *Finding a Voice*, Law Society Gazette, Sept. 21, 2006.

[53] Deaf Clients Get Free Sign Language Interpreters, Law Society PR, Oct. 31, 2005.

[54] Amir A. Majid, *Jury Still Out on Deaf Jurors*, 154 New L.J. 278-279, (Feb. 27, 2004) (the author is grateful to the Editor of the New Law Journal for permitting him to use parts of this article in this publication).

As a p.t Immigration Judge, the author is a member of the "Ministerial Reference Group" on Disability Equality in the Judiciary. This Group is headed by the Department of Constitutional Affairs Minister, Ms Harriet Harman, QC, and is currently involved in substantial progressive work. The UK PM, Tony Blair, may be in bad books of many people for his support of the US action in Iraq and Afghanistan but he cannot be denuded of the credit for the progressive measures he is taking to improve the fate of disabled people, particularly in the DCA at the ministerial level. Some policies are already adopted and enforced, if the group kept on working with present potency, this author hopes a lot to be changed for the better for disabled people in the fields of accessibility of court buildings, legal services, recruitment and training of law professionals and selection, appointment and support of disabled judges.

After receiving Royal Assent on 7 April 2005, the UK Disability Discrimination Act 2005 (amending the Disability Discrimination Act 1995) imposed a general duty by S.3 (1) on every public authority in the UK to accord equal treatment to people with sensory and/or physical disabilities. It imposes a mandatory duty on public authorities to "eliminate unlawful discrimination", prevent "harassment of disabled people", promote "equal opportunities for disabled people", promote "positive attitude towards disabled persons" and promote "participation of disabled people in public life." This legal obligation is dubbed as the "disability equality duty" (DED) which came into force on 4 December 2006. Section 3 (1) (d) is the most important legal protection promulgated hitherto in the UK. The authorities are obliged to take steps for achieving these goals, "even where that involves treating disabled persons more favourably than other persons."

CORPORATE GOVERNANCE IN AN EMERGING MARKET: A PERSPECTIVE ON PAKISTAN

Haroon H. Hamid[*] & Valeria Kozhich[**]

I) PREFACE

In March 2006, the Case Team on Corporate Governance in Pakistan (Case Team) held meetings in Islamabad and Karachi with senior officials from the Ministry of Finance, the Securities and Exchange Commission of Pakistan, the Ministry of Law, Justice & Human Rights, the State Bank of Pakistan, the Karachi Stock Exchange, the Central Depository Company, JCR-VIS Credit Rating Company, the Sindh High Court, publicly listed companies, banks, the financial press, and law firms involved in corporate governance. Case Team members in attendance were Haroon H. Hamid and Valeria Kozhich. The report was supervised by Professor Richard Gordon of Case Western Reserve University School of Law. The Case Team would especially like to thank Kausar Faridi, Resident Director of Direct Consulting Worldwide Inc., and Zakir Jaffer, Executive Director of Ahmed Jaffer & Co., for their invaluable assistance in Karachi and Islamabad.

The goal of this report is to assess corporate governance practices in Pakistan relative to the investment environment that members of the IIF Equity Advisory Group would like to see in emerging market countries. This report is not meant to provide exhaustive due diligence of corporate governance in Pakistan and neither the Case Team nor the IIF can in any way attest to or guarantee the accuracy or completeness of the information in this report.

II) KEY CORPORATE GOVERNANCE ISSUES

a) Overview of Corporate Governance in Pakistan

Corporate governance has recently taken center stage in Pakistan's business community. The principal source of corporate governance law is the Code of Corporate Governance ("Code"), which was first drafted by the Institute of Chartered Accountants of Pakistan ("ICAP") in 1998.[1] The Securities and Exchange Commission of Pakistan ("SECP") promulgated the Code in 2002.[2]

---

[*] B.S. 2002 (University of Michigan); J.D. 2006 (Case Western Reserve University School of Law). Mr. Hamid received a B.S. in Computer Science and Economics in 2002. He completed his Juris Doctorate, with an honor's concentration in International Law, in May 2006. Mr. Hamid's recent work experience includes a legal externship with the Honorable Federal District Judge John M. Manos and an internship at Nurenberg, Paris, Heller & McCarthy Co. LPA.

[**] B.S. 2003 (Georgetown University Edmund A. Walsh School of Foreign Service); J.D. 2006 (Case Western Reserve University School of Law). Ms. Kozhich received her B.S. in Foreign Service in 2003. She completed her Juris Doctorate, with an honor's concentration in International Law, in May 2006. Ms. Kozhich's work experience includes nanotechnology research at the Woodrow Wilson International Center for Scholars in Washington, D.C. and a legal internship at the Office of the Attorney General of the District of Columbia.

[1] Securities and Exchange Commission of Pakistan, Code of Corporate Governance, Mar 2002, http://www.ecgi.org/codes/documents/code_corporate(revised).pdf, [hereinafter Code of Corporate Governance].

[2] Id.

Corporate governance is also covered in the Companies Ordinance of 1984[3] ("Companies Ordinance") and the Banking Companies Ordinance of 1962.[4]

Presently, corporate governance primarily falls within the ambit of two entities: the SECP and the State Bank of Pakistan ("SBP"). The SECP, which was formed in 1997 by legislative action, is the chief enforcer of the Code.[5] While the SECP's predecessor, the Corporate Law Authority, was a division of the Ministry of Finance and under the Ministry's control, the SECP is largely an independent body that regulates the corporate sector and capital markets.[6] The SECP also regulates non-banking financial institutions.[7] The Ministry of Finance retains the authority to appoint the SECP's commissioners.[8] The commissioners are typically top professionals involved in capital markets and many of them come from the private sector. The SECP's autonomy is encouraging as the independence of a regulator is increasingly important for good corporate governance. Most importantly for corporate governance, the SECP enforces the listing requirements for the three stock exchanges of Pakistan: the Karachi Stock Exchange ("KSE"), the Lahore Stock Exchange ("LSE"), and the Islamabad Stock Exchange ("ISE").[9] Since the Code's provisions are incorporated into the listing requirements of the exchanges, the SECP ensures compliance with those requirements.

The SBP is Pakistan's central bank and is responsible for regulating the country's banking and finance sector.[10] The SBP has the authority to enforce corporate governance guidelines for banks. In addition to complying with the Code, banks must comply with the Prudential Regulations of the SBP and the Banking Ordinance of 1962. However, regulations for banks are more stringent and detailed than those for other listed companies and are beyond the scope of this report.

The entities responsible for the implementation and enforcement of corporate governance in Pakistan are illustrated below:

---

[3] The Companies Ordinance 1984, http://www.secp.gov.pk/corporatelaws/nov_30_00.htm.
[4] Banking Companies Ordinance 1962, as amended up to May 31st, 1997, http://www.sbp.org.pk/publications/prudential/ordinance_62.pdf.
[5] Securities and Exchange Commission of Pakistan, Establishment of Securities and Exchange Commission of Pakistan, http://www.secp.gov.pk/aboutus.htm (last visited Dec. 1, 2006).
[6] Information of Pakistan, http://www.pak.gov.pk/register-company.aspx (last visited Dec. 2, 2006).
[7] Securities and Exchange Commission of Pakistan, *supra* note 5.
[8] *See id.*
[9] *Id.*
[10] State Bank of Pakistan, http://www.sbp.org.pk/about/index.asp (last visited Dec. 1, 2006).

```
┌─────────────────────────────────┐
│      Ministry of Finance        │
│                                 │
│  ▪ No longer has direct control │
│    over the operations of the   │
│    autonomous SECP              │
│  ▪ Selects the SECP's           │
│    commissioners                │
└─────────────────────────────────┘
```

┌──────────────────────────────┐   ┌──────────────────────────────┐
│   SECP   │   │   SBP   │
│   │   │   │
│ ▪ Regulates the corporate   │   │ ▪ Regulates the banking and │
│   sector and capital markets │   │   financial sector   │
│ ▪ Supervises the stock   │   │ ▪ Supervises banks and has   │
│   exchanges and has authority│   │   ultimate authority to   │
│   over listed companies   │   │   penalize and restructure   │
│   through stock exchange   │   │   non-conforming banks   │
│   listing requirements   │   │   │
└──────────────────────────────┘   └──────────────────────────────┘

b) Predominance of Family-Controlled Corporations

Pakistani corporations have been historically family-controlled, especially those in the textile, automotive, tobacco, and agricultural sectors. Today, the majority of corporations in Pakistan remain under family control. There are three main types of listed corporations in Pakistan: multinational, family-controlled, and state-owned enterprises ("SOE"). A majority of listed corporations are family-controlled via pyramid structures and cross-shareholdings.

A trend of altering the family-controlled structure of corporations has emerged. One factor in this trend is the increased awareness by many corporations of the need for good governance. Another is the return of new graduates of U.S. and UK educational institutions to their family-controlled businesses. These graduates bring new insight and realize that to compete globally and to maximize value; Pakistani corporations must change their governance structures. Yet, there remains an uphill battle against the "old school" of family control and a rubber stamp board. A fundamental misgiving among the majority of family-controlled companies is the idea that ceding control and diversifying the board is inimical to their interests. Further education on the advantages of a diversified board structure is necessary to change this misconception.

c) Pakistan's Equity Culture

Pakistan's equity culture is still developing. The lack of focus on an equity culture in the 1980s, the high returns on government bonds and easy access to bank loans in the 1990s all discouraged an equity culture in Pakistan.[11] Debt financing is still prevalent, which hinders further development of an equity culture. The equity market is relatively shallow and is oriented mostly towards a handful of major companies. According to ICAP, Pakistan's equity market was

---

[11] *See* Nasim Beg, Building an Equity Culture in Pakistan: Risk Management Through Mutual Funds, Presented at the Institute of Chartered Accountants of Pakistan, Feb. 2005, http://www.icap.org.pk/Downloads/Seminars/%20ICAP.ppt.

40% of its GDP in 2005.[12] Current reforms on the government's agenda are the demutualization of the stock exchanges and the creation of over-the-counter markets, both of which will help increase the depth of the market.

The KSE is the largest of the three equity markets in Pakistan[13] and has been one of the best performing markets in the world over the past 4 years.[14] Currently there are 663 listed companies on the KSE with a total market capitalization of approximately US$54 billion.[15]

However, equity financing is still not a priority because of a lack of competition in various industries. Family-controlled companies are often satisfied with their position in the market and prefer not to risk weakening family control by selling shares to minority investors.

d) The Code of Corporate Governance

The present Code is a diluted version of the original drafted by ICAP in 1998. In preparing the Code, the drafters examined international models of corporate governance. These include the Cadbury Committee Report and Hampbell Committee Report from the UK, in addition to the King's Report from South Africa. The Code is mandatory for listed companies, although some of the most important provisions, such as the requirement to have independent directors, are still voluntary. An exciting feature of the Code is that there is a "checklist" of what is mandatory and voluntary, which makes it easy to determine a company's compliance with the Code.

The Code is a "comply or explain" document. The Case Team's discussions with government officials revealed that the Code was intentionally left as a "comply or explain" document because of the general lack of education about corporate governance at the time of the Code's implementation. The idea was to take the first steps towards good corporate governance by familiarizing people with the concept. Once people were more aware of corporate governance and its ramifications, it would then be easier to make the Code more than just a "comply or explain" system. A revision of the Code may be forthcoming soon because of the recent increase in awareness of good corporate governance.

i) Independent Directors under the Code of Corporate Governance

The Code provides for "[r]epresentation of independent non-executive directors, including those representing minority interests, on the Board of Directors of listed companies."[16] This provision, however, is one of two voluntary provisions in the code.[17] Thus, although the Code is mandatory for listed companies, the companies do not have to follow the provision that is of the utmost importance to the minority equity investor. The proportion of independent directors on a board is also not specified.

Although "independent" is defined, the definition is fairly broad and leaves plenty of room for competing interpretations. Moreover, the definition of "independent" does not address minority shareholder rights. The definition states:

> Independent director means a director who is not connected with the listed company, or its promoters, or directors, on the basis of family relationship and who does not have any

---

[12] *Id.*

[13] Rajendar Menen, *Promising Performance*, GULF NEWS REPORT, Aug. 13, 2006, http://www.gulfnews.com/supplements/pakistan2006/sub_story/10059848.html.

[14] Naween A. Mangi, *And World's Top Market Is . . . Pakistan*, BUSINESSWEEK ONLINE, Apr. 10, 2003, http://www.businessweek.com/bwdaily/dnflash/apr2003/nf20030410_4232_db039.htm?chan=search.

[15] Rajendar Menen, *supra* note 13.

[16] Code of Corporate Governance, *supra* note 1.

[17] *Id.*

other relationship, whether pecuniary or otherwise, with the listed company, its associated companies, directors, executives or related parties. The test of independence principally emanates from the fact whether such person can be reasonably perceived as being able to exercise independent business judgment without being subservient to any apparent form of interference.[18]

The definition does not specify the type of family relationship addressed – someone as distant as a third cousin could be considered non-independent because of an extremely attenuated family relationship. The definition should not be so broad as to render it meaningless and to exclude almost every qualified individual.[19] Further, "any other relationship"[20] is so vague that it offers minimal guidance on who should be an independent director.[21]

The fact that the Code's definition does not mention minority shareholder interests and that the provision itself is voluntary is troubling for minority equity investors. Minority shareholder representation by independent directors is one of the main methods for a minority shareholder investing in an emerging market to protect its interests in a corporation. The voluntary nature of this provision in a mandatory, albeit comply or explain code, indicates that minority shareholder protection is not yet valued highly in the Pakistani corporate sector.

The Companies Ordinance defines minority shareholders as shareholders that together hold at least 20% of the company's equity share.[22] At least 20% equity share is required for a minority shareholder to bring a suit in the courts.[23] Pakistan has a few large government-run pension funds, however, the proportion of what they own prevents them from championing minority shareholder rights like similar funds in the U.S. Even those funds that own the required 20%, are generally passive. Thus, corporate governance as it exists in Pakistan today is geared mainly towards reigning in the majority rather than protecting the minority.

e) Effects of the Code of Corporate Governance

i) Voluntary Compliance

A number of corporations are currently complying with the Code. The Case Team determined during the course of its interviews with various entities that good corporate governance is a key issue that is foremost in the mind of many executives. An example is the Central Depository Company ("CDC"), which is in charge of the Central Depository System – the clearinghouse for the three stock exchanges in Pakistan.[24] The CDC is one of Pakistan's "shining stars" of corporate governance – it voluntarily complied with the Code despite not being listed. The CDC complied because of its desire to be the best company possible and to be a role model for various entities, especially for those companies listed on the stock exchanges. The ability to attract foreign capital was not the driving factor. Furthermore, many companies follow the Code in preparation for becoming listed. Voluntary compliance is a positive sign because it demonstrates that people are becoming more aware of the role that corporate governance plays in a successful corporation.

---

[18] *Id.*
[19] *Id.*
[20] *Id.*
[21] *Id.*
[22] The Companies Ordinance 1984, *supra* note 3.
[23] *Id.*
[24] About CDC Pakistan, http://www.cdcpakistan.com/about.htm#Introduction (last visited Dec. 2, 2006).

ii) De-listing

Some companies have voluntarily de-listed after the Code came into effect. In 2001, before the Code was implemented, the number of companies listed on the KSE was 747.[25] In 2006, four years after the Code went into effect, only 663 companies are listed.[26] The Case Team heard differing accounts during its interviews about the reasons for de-listing. Some interviewees suggested that companies de-listed solely as a result of the Code while others suggested that although the Code may have played a factor, it would not have been the primary motivator for de-listing. A common complaint about the Code is the increased cost of frequent financial reporting required by the Code, especially the quarterly unaudited statements. Several majority family-controlled companies de-listed because the cost of compliance did not justify the minimal minority shareholding in their companies. Many such companies did not want to incur the cost of restructuring just to accommodate one person on a twelve member board. Such resistance to change demonstrates that the concept of the minority investor is lacking.

f) Corporate Governance in State-owned Enterprises ("SOEs")

A common complaint is that SOEs are held to a lower standard than other listed companies. Most SOEs do not currently follow the provisions of the Code. Market data on SOEs is hard to find, but the number of SOEs currently existing is approximately 150. However, new regulations are being promulgated to create a corporate governance code targeted specifically towards SOEs.

A SOE-specific code is particularly important for Pakistan because a number of key companies are state-owned. Pakistan International Airlines, the largest airline in Pakistan, is a state-owned enterprise with an 88% government share. Many entities in the gas and power sector are also state-owned. The government, however, has been steadily privatizing SOEs and selling them to the public through the exchanges. From 1988 to 1995, the revenue from privatizations was approximately US$ 1.5 billion. The privatization of the Pakistan Telecommunications Company Ltd ("PTCL") was one of the government's main privatization activities in 2005. Etisalat, a telecommunications company headquartered in the United Arab Emirates, acquired 26% of PTCL's shares when privatization began.[27] Privatization is important because an SOE often does not have a chairman appointed by the Board or market-based compensation for its directors. The ability to appoint a chairman and the compensation of directors are both necessary for effective corporate governance. Another benefit of privatization is improved liquidity.

The wisdom of having a completely separate corporate governance code for SOEs is debatable. It is arguably better to have one general code with specific provisions applicable only to SOEs. Such a code would resolve the issue of having a fragmented corporate governance law by consolidating the law in one place. Consequently, the requirements would not only be easier to follow but also easier to police.

g) Obstacles to Good Corporate Governance

i) Lack of Penal Provisions in the Code of Corporate Governance

There are no penal provisions in the Code and hence deterrence is limited. A number of people the Case Team interviewed believed that the addition of penal provisions would make the Code more effective in establishing good corporate governance. Compliance with the Code is

---

[25] KARACHI STOCK EXCHANGE, ANNUAL REPORT 6 (2005).
[26] Rajendar Menen, *supra* note 13.
[27] *Deal signed to give Etisalat PTCL control*, DAWN, March 13, 2006, http://www.dawn.com/2006/03/13/top5.htm.

construed loosely because all that is necessary is an annual statement of compliance verified by an auditor. In the Code's "comply or explain" regime, an auditor simply verifies a statement provided by the company, which itself indicates what areas of the Code it has followed, without necessarily verifying the accuracy of the information.

However, penal provisions are an *ex post* mechanism that do not protect the interests of minority shareholders until it is too late. Moreover, penalizing a company will often translate into penalties for the minority shareholders, since they have a stake in that company.

ii) The Financial Press Does Not Actively Deter Bad Corporate Governance

The Pakistani financial press does not provide active deterrence, and as such fails to provide the additional level of enforcement necessary for good corporate governance. The financial press often plays an important role in promoting good corporate governance, especially where traditional enforcement mechanisms are lacking or are ineffective. Thus, an active financial press that keeps shareholders abreast of company developments is vital to minority shareholder protection.

The Pakistani business community feels that the Pakistani financial press is still developing and is not as active as it could be. At least two English financial newspapers are widely circulated among the business community. Although major domestic and international corporate developments are widely reported, a common complaint is the effectiveness of the Pakistani financial press in actively pursuing corporate matters. The papers do not actively provide routine yet important information to shareholders, but rather focus on major stories and scandals.

In addition, there have been failures of due diligence in the Pakistani financial press. One such failure caused a drastic decline in the KSE in March 2006. The KSE, which was hovering around 11,000 points dropped some 400 points in one day when a leading financial newspaper reported that foreign shareholders would have to declare their holdings to the government. Later it was discovered that this information was taken out of context and not appropriately verified by the newspaper. Consequently, a number of foreign investors pulled out of the market causing a precipitous drop in the KSE, which is still vulnerable to such rumors.

The television media is better at active deterrence than the financial press. Several financial news channels have appeared in Pakistan in the past few years. The competition to get the latest story is fierce and even foreign financial channels have established local channels to stake out a share of this growing sector. The most recent entrant is CNBC Pakistan, which transmits business news from across the country 24/7 in both Urdu and English. These networks provide pertinent and up-to-date information on the markets.

iii) Lack of Active Monitoring by the SECP

The "comply or explain" regime in place in Pakistan does not give the SECP an active monitoring role – listed companies just need their statement of compliance signed by a verified accountant. Accordingly, many companies think of the Code as simply requiring a rubber stamp, not any serious compliance. A more active monitoring system, balanced between too much interference and no monitoring, would help ensure greater compliance with the Code. A major complaint the Case Team heard was that the stock exchanges themselves do not completely follow the Code. Recently, however, the SECP appeared to be moving towards more vigorous enforcement of the Code. For example, it placed four independent directors on the KSE's board of directors to bring the KSE in compliance with the Code.

iv) Weak Legal System

The legal system provides little effective recourse for any shareholder, let alone the minority shareholder whose rights have been violated. The court system is overburdened, plagued with delays and suffers from a general lack of experience with corporate matters.[28] However, reforms have been introduced to improve the ability of the court system to handle such matters. The High Courts of Pakistan's four provinces are required to have a companies judge to handle corporate matters. All foreign investors and local investors with a threshold capital investment can bring their claims directly to the High Courts, without going through the lengthy process of bringing their claim before the lower courts and then waiting for it to reach the High Courts. As such, the High Courts have original jurisdiction on those matters. Although steps are being taken to create a more accommodating legal system, the largely lethargic system does not present a positive outlook for minority investors in the short to medium term.

v) Remuneration of Directors

Despite the voluntary nature of the requirement for independent directors, many companies, including those that are not required to comply with the Code, have appointed independent directors. However, people willing to serve as independent directors are difficult to find because remuneration is not commensurate with the duties or liabilities of directors. Even though there are qualified candidates, there is little incentive for them to subject themselves to the liability inherent in such a position without being compensated accordingly. A market-based remuneration scheme will attract qualified directors who will be willing to take on the responsibilities and liabilities of such a position.

vi) Corporate Governance Law is Fragmented

Although the Code was recently promulgated in 2002, certain corporate governance provisions remain only in the Companies Ordinance.[29] The Companies Ordinance deals directly with the protection of minority shareholders. For example, a company can be wound up by the court if it "conduct[s] its business in a manner oppressive to . . . the minority shareholders."[30] As a result, many corporations initially resisted the Code because there were already several laws in effect pertaining to corporate governance. Often these laws are more stringent than the Code itself. To facilitate the implementation of sound corporate governance, it may be easier to have the Code cross-reference the Companies Ordinance for certain provisions.

h) Prospects for Better Corporate Governance

i) Exit Option for Minority Shareholders During a Merger

An exit option for minority shareholders during a merger provides minority shareholders with the ability to exit when the risk structure changes and there is a high chance that company management could change. Under a recent takeover ordinance, there is an exit option for minority shareholders in the event of a buyout or merger of a listed company. Additionally, acquisition of 10% or more of voting shares requires public disclosure, followed by a tender offer. In such a case, the SECP retains the authority to re-value exit shares. A recent example involved a leading company that was trading on the KSE at Rs. 10 per share. After the company was acquired, the SECP determined that the company's shares were undervalued. Thus, the SECP revalued the shares resulting in a new value of Rs. 100 per share for minority shareholders

---

[28] Syed Mohammad Ali, *VIEW: Increasing access to justice*, DAILY TIMES, Oct. 17, 2006, http://www.dailytimes.com.pk/default.asp?page=2006%5C10%5C17%5Cstory_17-10-2006_pg3_5.

[29] Code of Corporate Governance, *supra* note 1.

[30] The Companies Ordinance 1984, *supra* note 3.

looking to exit. Since the SECP has the right to enquire into tender offers and make binding recommendations on what action the company should take, exiting minority shareholders were offered Rs. 100 per share.

ii) Education and Training in Corporate Governance

Companies in Pakistan, both small and large, and public and private, have become aware of corporate governance and its benefits. These include not only the future benefit of attracting foreign capital, but more importantly the benefit of developing robust corporate structures that are not easy prey for corruption and mismanagement.

The Lahore University of Management Sciences ("LUMS") – a top Pakistani business school – is actively working on improving corporate governance. LUMS created a corporate governance institute with funding from the Citigroup Foundation to encourage active dialogue on corporate governance issues and to develop good governance in Pakistan. The institute has been active in promoting corporate governance through annual conferences and case studies, in addition to researching the subject.

iii) Pakistan Institute of Corporate Governance

The Pakistan Institute of Corporate Governance is an initiative by ICAP – one of the pioneers of corporate governance in Pakistan – to educate directors on corporate governance issues and to improve the general understating of corporate governance in the business community and in government. The Institute should be operational within a few months.

iv) Government Initiatives and Support

The Pakistani government is aggressively promoting good corporate governance in Pakistan. Toward this end, the top posts at the Ministry of Finance, the SECP, and the SBP are staffed with professionals and individuals with private sector experience. Moreover, the government is taking a leading role in promoting corporate governance through initiatives for SOEs. A code of corporate governance targeted towards the state-owned sector of the Pakistani economy is forthcoming in Summer 2006.

v) Voluntary Compliance

Many unlisted small and large companies are complying with the Code even though compliance is only mandatory for listed companies. The general consensus on voluntary compliance is a desire to achieve an efficient board structure that minimizes insider transactions and increases a company's effectiveness. Thus, voluntary compliance is an encouraging indication that companies of all calibers are becoming aware of the significance of a well-governed company.

vi) Ratification of the New York Convention on the Recognition and Enforcement of Foreign Arbitral Awards

Although Pakistan has been a signatory to the New York Convention since 1958, it only recently ratified the Convention.[31] Consequently, while enforcement of foreign arbitral judgments may have been cumbersome in the past, the process should now be smoother. A burdened judicial system, however, may continue to be a bottleneck for such enforcement.

---

[31] UNCITRAL, Status, 1958 - Convention on the Recognition and Enforcement of Foreign Arbitral Awards, http://www.uncitral.org/uncitral/en/uncitral_texts/arbitration/NYConvention_status.html (last visited Jan. 6, 2007).

vii) Arbitration and Alternative Dispute Resolution

Arbitration is an effective alternative to the court system. Many companies use binding arbitration, which is cheaper and faster than litigation. However, arbitral decisions are final and cannot be appealed. Thus, other methods of dispute resolution such as mediation and negotiation may be viable alternatives.

viii) Anti-Corruption Measures

The National Accountability Bureau ("NAB") was commissioned by the government to investigate and prosecute criminal activity and mass corporate fraud.[32] While the NAB may be effective in apprehending major corporate criminals, it is primarily an *ex post* system that has been successful to some extent. For example, the system of lending in Pakistan was seen as sufficient to finance companies operating in the country. This was because of a network of connected lending and also because of loan defaults by major corporate players without recourse. Companies were allowed to default on large loans without penalties. NAB, via its exit control lists and stiff penalties, has improved the situation to a degree.

The development of a credit reporting system has also played an important role in holding borrowers accountable. In the past 5 years, Pakistan has gone from a country with a "credit reference" system to a system where individuals and corporations have their credit histories reported to a central system. Accordingly, lenders are less likely to have a defaulting obligation.

ix) Proactive Changes in the Law

Pakistan, like many developing countries, has generally been slow to update its companies laws. The legislature should take an aggressive approach to modernizing laws to accommodate the changing times and to provide checks against major corporate failures that have occurred worldwide. The Companies Ordinance is illustrative of this need to actively pursue changes in the law. The Company Law of 1913 was only updated in 1984[33] and has not been updated since (although there have been some amendments since the Code was promulgated in 2002).[34] Thus, the current Companies Ordinance even fails to take into account the changes in the nature of business brought about by the advent of the internet. Law makers should be flexible and change the law as necessary to keep the wheels of commerce turning.

III) PARTICIPANTS IN THE CASE TEAM CORPORATE GOVERNANCE PROJECT

Dr. Salman Shah Adviser to the Prime Minister of Pakistan for Finance, Revenue, and Economic Affairs *Ministry of Finance*	**Professor Richard K. Gordon, Esq.** Professor of Law Case Western Reserve University School of Law
Mr. Omar Ayub Khan	**Mr. Humayun L. Hamid**

---

[32] National Accountability Bureau, About Us, http://www.nab.gov.pk/index.asp (last visited Dec. 11, 2006).

[33] Shamim Ahmad Khan, Former Chairman, Securities and Exchange Commission of Pakistan, *Business Registration Reforms in Pakistan*, Apr 23, 2004, http://0-siteresources.worldbank.org.library.vu.edu.au/INTWDR2005/Resources/477407-1096581040435/wdr2005_pakistan_business_registration_reforms2.pdf.

[34] *See id.*

Minister of State
Ministry of Finance

Mr. Rana Assad Amin
Joint Secretary
Ministry of Finance

Mr. Razi-ur-Rahman Khan
Chairman
Securities & Exchange Commission of Pakistan

Dr. Sajid Qureshi
Executive Director
Securities & Exchange Commission of Pakistan

Mr. Waseem Ahmad Khan
Deputy Registrar of Companies, Company Law Division
Securities & Exchange Commission of Pakistan

Mr. Tariq Bakhtawar
Director, Enforcement
Securities & Exchange Commission of Pakistan

Mr. Jameel Ahmad
Director, Banking Supervision Department
State Bank of Pakistan

Ms. Kausar Faridi
Resident Director
Direct Consulting Worldwide Inc.

Mr. Faheem Ahmad
President & CEO
JCR-VIS Credit Rating Company Limited

Mr. Saad Ahmed Madani
Group Head – Corporate & Structured Finance
JCR-VIS Credit Rating Company Limited

Mr. Farrukh V. Junaidy
Chief Financial Officer
Dewan Mushtaq Group

Mr. Tariq Muhammad Khan
Director Treasury & Commercial
Dewan Mushtaq Group

Mr. Zafar Abdullah
Chief Compliance Officer

Chairman
Hamid Group of Companies

Mr. Zakir Jaffer
Executive Director
Ahmed Jaffer & Co.

Mr. Mohammed Yasin Lakhani
Former Chairman
The Karachi Stock Exchange (Guarantee) Limited

Mr. M.A. Lodhi
Managing Director
The Karachi Stock Exchange (Guarantee) Limited

Mr. Muhammed Yacoob Memon
Deputy Managing Director
The Karachi Stock Exchange (Guarantee) Limited

Mr. Haroon Askari
Chief Manager Operations
The Karachi Stock Exchange (Guarantee) Limited

Mr. Asif Ali Rashid
Chairman
Sigma Leasing Corporation Limited

Mr. Mohammed Hanif Jakhura
Chief Executive Officer
Central Depository Company of Pakistan Limited

Mr. Kamran Ahmed Qazi
Head of Finance & Company Secretary
Central Depository Company of Pakistan Limited

Mr. Raja Qasit Nawaz Khan
Advocate High Court
Raja Haq Nawaz Khan Law Associates

Mr. Abdul R. Sattar
Attorney-at-Law
Sattar and Sattar

Mr. Irfan Mohsin Tayebaly
Partner
Mohsin Tayebaly & Co.

Dewan Mushtaq Group

Mr. Syed Moonis Abdullah Alvi
Senior General Manager Treasury & Commercial
Dewan Mushtaq Group

Mr. Irfan Ahmed Qureshi
General Manager (Finance)
Baluchistan Wheels Limited

Mr. Mansoor Ali Khan
Authorized Representative in Pakistan
Interscan

Ms. Qudsia Kadri Khan
CEO & Editor-in-Chief
The Financial Post

Mr. Athar Zaheer Rizvi
Company Secretary
NIB Bank

Mr. Yameen Kerai
Chief Financial Officer
NIB Bank

Mr. M. Siddique Memon
SVP, Company Secretary & Legal Advisor
Faysal Bank

Mr. Ruhail Mohammed
Chief Financial Officer
Engro Chemical Pakistan Ltd.

Mr. Andalib Alavi
General Manager – Legal & Company Secretary
Engro Chemical Pakistan Ltd.

Mr. Akbar Abdullah
Vice President
The Federation of Pakistan Chambers of Commerce & Industry

Mr. Muhammad Iqbal Tabish
Director, Research & Economic Development
The Federation of Pakistan Chambers of Commerce & Industry

RECONSIDERING REGULATION: A HISTORICAL VIEW OF THE LEGALITY OF INTERNET POKER AND DISCUSSION OF THE INTERNET GAMBLING BAN OF 2006

Christopher Grohman[*][┌]

I) INTRODUCTION

It's the hottest new thing in sports. George Steinbrenner, outspoken owner of perpetual World Series contenders the New York Yankees, admonished his star shortstop, Alex Rodriguez, to stop playing it.[1] Former NBA all-star and basketball hall of fame-nominee Charles Barkley plays it recreationally.[2] Yevgeny Kafelnikov, former winner of both the Australian and the French tennis Opens, is now considered a professional player.[3] Hollywood actors Ben Affleck[4] and Tobey McGuire are taking lessons[5] and Academy Award nominee Jennifer Tilly recently won a world championship in it.[6]

No, I am not referring to the American revival of soccer: I am talking about poker—more specifically, "Texas Hold'Em Poker."[7] Noted poker author Jim McManus estimated that in 2001

---

[*] Christopher Grohman is a graduate of both the Wharton School of Business and Harvard Law School. Currently, he is a federal law clerk in the Southern District of Ohio. You can also find him at $20-$40 stud games across the country.

[┌] Many thanks to Professor Charles Nesson, founder of the Berkman Center for Internet at Society at Harvard Law School, and Daniel Walsh of Greenberg Traurig for their help and guidance on this paper. Lastly, many thanks and my undying admiration to Ndidi Anyaegbunam, without whom, this paper, and many other things, would be lost forever.

1. Associated Press, *Yankees Tell A-Rod to Avoid Illegal Poker Clubs*, ESPN NEWS, November 2, 2005, http://sports.espn.go.com/mlb/news/story?id=2211201 [hereinafter AROD].
2. *Everybody Loves Brad Garett*, *Magazine Archives*, BLUFF MAGAZINE, October, 2005, http://www.bluffmagazine.com/magazine/2005_10_72.asp
3. *Biography: Yevgeny Kaelnikov*, http://www.answers.com/topic/yevgeny-kafelnikov
4. Associated Press, *Ben Affleck Poker King*, CBS NEWS ONLINE, June 22, 2004, http://www.cbsnews.com/stories/2004/06/22/entertainment/main625235.shtml
5. *See* Phil Hellmuth, *Spider-Man Can Play*, CARDPLAYER MAGAZINE Volume 17 No. 25, December 3, 2004; Poker professional Phil Hellmuth comments of the increasing progress Tobey McGuire has made after taking lessons with him.
6. James Joyner, *Actress Jennifer Tilly Wins World Series of Poker*, OUTSIDE THE BELTWAY, June 29, 2005, http://www.outsidethebeltway.com/archives/2005/06/actress_jennifer_tilly_wins_world_series_of_poker/
7. *See* http://en.wikipedia.org/wiki/Texas_hold%27em. "Texas hold 'em (often referred to as simply "hold'em") is the most popular of the community card poker games as of 2006. It is also the most popular poker variant played in casinos in the United States, and its no-limit betting form is used in the main event of the World Series of Poker (WSOP), as seen on ESPN, widely recognized as the world championship of the game. It is also the main game in the World Poker Tour (WPT) that hosts international poker tournaments around the globe. Play begins with each player being dealt two cards face down. These cards are the player's hole cards. These are the only cards each player will receive individually, and they will only (possibly) be revealed at the showdown, making Texas hold 'em a closed poker game. The hand begins with a "pre-flop" betting round, beginning with the player to the left of the big blind (or the player to the left of the dealer, if no blinds are used) and continuing clockwise. After the

there were between 60 and 80 million poker players in the United States,[8] and the numbers have only increased since then. It is hard to turn on ESPN without seeing a televised poker tournament or an advertisement for an upcoming one. Nowhere has the increasing popularity of poker been more evident than at the World Series of Poker (WSOP). The WSOP is an annual series of poker tournaments usually held in Las Vegas in late July or early August. Entry is available to anyone who pays an entrance fee. These fees range from $500 for some of the smaller events to $10,000 for the main event. The entrance fees are combined to form the prize pool. The winner of the tournament typically receives 25 percent of the prize pool and lower finishers receive less; typically, only the top 10 percent of finishers receive a portion of the prize pool.[9]

The WSOP was started in 1970 by Benny Binion, owner and manager of Binion's Horseshoe Casino in Las Vegas, Nevada.[10] The first WSOP tournament was held in 1971 and had only 7 entrants.[11] Now owned by Harrahs,[12] the most recent WSOP was held at the Rio Hotel and Casino in 2006.[13] The tournament had 45 events and the main event had 8,773 registered participants.[14] The amount of prize money has also increased dramatically; the first place prize for the main event was $30,000 in 1971, a mere pittance when compared to the $12 million awarded in 2006.[15] To put this figure in prospective, the $12 million prize represents the largest payout in the history of sporting events, more than 3 times the combined prizes of the 2006 Masters Golf Tournament and the 2006 US Open tennis tournament.[16]

The massive prize money and record number of entrants in the WSOP is even more staggering when viewed in light of their recent increases. For example, in 2002, the WSOP main event had only 631 entrants. There was nearly a 1400 percent increase from 2002 to 2006.

---

pre-flop betting round, the dealer deals a burn card, followed by three face-up community cards called the flop. The flop is followed by a second betting round. This and all subsequent betting rounds begin with the player to the dealer's left and continue clockwise. After the flop betting round ends, another card is burned, and a single community card called the turn (or fourth street) is dealt, followed by a third betting round. A final burn card is followed by a single community card called the river (or fifth street), followed by a fourth betting round and the showdown, if necessary. Betting structures: In casino play, it is common to use a fixed limit and two blinds. The limit for the first two rounds of betting is called a small bet, while the limit for the third and fourth betting rounds is called a big bet and is generally double the small bet. In casino and most tournament play, a professional dealer who is not a player in the game deals the cards. A dealer button is used to represent the player in the dealer position; the dealer button rotates clockwise after each hand, changing the postion of the dealer and blinds. The small blind is posted by the player to the left of the dealer and is usually equal to half of a small bet, and the big blind, posted by the player to the left of the small blind, is equal to a full small bet. After the flop one can bet an amount equal to the big bling, after the turn and the river one can bet or raise two big blinds. Most tournaments use a no-limit structure where a player may be any amount at any time."

[8]. See JIM MCMANUS, POSITIVELY FIFTH STREET (Farrar, Straus, and Giroux, 2003).
[9]. See generally http://en.wikipedia.org/wiki/World_Series_of_Poker and http://en.wikipedia.org/wiki/2006_WSOP [herinafter WikiWSOP]
[10]. Id.
[11]. Id.
[12]. See id. Harrahs bought out Binion's and the rights to the WSOP in 2005.
[13]. Id.
[14]. Id.
[15]. See WikiWSOP, supra note 9.
[16]. See http://www.chiff.com/a/us-open-tickets.htm and http://www.augusta.com/masters/history/leaderboards/2006leaderboard.shtml respectively.

Two significant factors that caused the sudden emergence of poker in the mainstream of American pop-culture: first, the televised broadcasts of major poker tournaments; and second, Chris Moneymaker, an "every-man," winning the 2003 WSOP main event.[17]

Poker's popularity is reflected by the television coverage devoted to it, as poker tournaments are carried by at least four channels. ESPN covers the WSOP, the Travel Channel broadcasts the newly developed World Poker Tour (WPT), NBC shows the National Heads-Up Poker Championship, and Fox Sports Net televises various other poker events.[18] It is not simply the televising of poker that caused its boom, but more the innovations in poker televising. ESPN actually began broadcasting the WSOP in the mid-1980s, but because very few hands involved players showing their cards to the audience face up, the televised event had little entertainment value for viewers. It was, as WSOP director of operations Gary Thompson put it, "as fun as watching paint dry."[19] This changed in 2003, when ESPN began using the "pocket-cam," a small camera inserted in the sides of the poker table that enables viewers to see each player's "down-cards" (cards that are unexposed to the other players at the table). This allows viewers to see each player's cards and play along with the game, making watching the event more engaging. With the advent of the pocket-cam, ESPN expanded its coverage from a one-hour encapsulation of the main event, to a series that spans almost two months and contains slice-of-life profiles on various players.[20]

The second cause of the poker explosion was Tennessee accountant Chris Moneymaker's victory in the 2003 WSOP main event. Moneymaker won his $10,000 entry fee through a series of smaller tournaments held on an online poker site[21] which he entered for a fee of only $40. Prior to Moneymaker's win, professional players dominated WSOP events.[22] The victory of Moneymaker, a novice, made the dream of winning these major tournaments tangible to recreational players everywhere. Since his victory, there has been an increase in the number of amateur players competing in the event, and two non-professional players, Greg "Fossilman" Raymer, an attorney from Connecticut, and Joseph Hachem, a former chiropractor from Australia, have won the WSOP main event.[23]

Many media related organizations, such as the World Poker Tour, are trying to capture the revenue generated by the increasing popularity of poker. On May 20, 2002, a newly formed company called the World Poker Tour, LLC ("WPT") announced its launch into the burgeoning world of televised upscale poker tournaments. The WPT was founded by Stephen Lipscomb, an attorney and television producer. In its first season, the WPT hosted 13 $10,000+ buy-in tournaments at casinos throughout the country. The casinos keep a small portion of the players' entrance fees and the WPT makes money from a television deal with the Travel Channel as well as from various advertising sources.[24] Since 2002, the WPT has expanded rapidly and will have 44 televised events in 2006.[25] Other television shows, such as Celebrity Poker[26] shown on the

---

[17] See WikiWSOP, supra note 9.
[18] THE POKER FORUM, http://www.thepokerforum.com/pokerontv.htm
[19] http://www.pokerplayernewspaper.com/pokerlore.php
[20] See WikiWSOP, supra note 9.
[21] See www.Pokerstars.com
[22] See Chris Moneymakers website, http://www.chrismoneymaker.com/poker/bio/
[23] See WikiWSOP, supra note 9.
[24] See http://www.pokernews.com/news/2005/12/wpt-ceo-lipscomb-open-letter.htm
[25] See generally http://www.pokerpages.com/newsletter/articles/world-poker-tour01.htm and http://en.wikipedia.org/wiki/World_Poker_Tour (last visited May 18, 2006)
[26] See Bravo's website, http://www.bravotv.com/Celebrity_Poker_Showdown/. The show consists of 6 B-list celebrities playing Texas Hold'em where the winner receives a monetary award for the charity

Bravo network and Poker Stars Invitational on Fox Sports Net, have sprung up in the wake of the WPT's success. Television clearly has fueled America's obsession with high stakes poker.

America's heightened interest in poker, especially amongst 18–29 year-olds, has caused the rise of a new profitable industry—online poker. Since 2002, online poker sites have become a powerful presence in the online gambling market. These sites allow anyone with an Internet connection to download a program that enables them to play poker with other players anywhere in the world.

Players can choose from a wide variety of poker games on these sites—Texas Hold'Em, Omaha Hold'Em, Omaha High-Low, 7 Card Stud, and others. Players use their credit or debit cards[27] to deposit money on the site.[28] Then, just like cash at a casino, players exchange this money for virtual chips. They can then win or lose virtual chips at the poker tables with their winnings being credited to their account on the poker site and their losses being deducted; if they lose their whole deposit, they must deposit more money to continue playing.

These sites make money in the same way as brick and mortar casino poker rooms—through a concept called the "rake."[29] In a cash game, the rake is generally ten percent of the amount wagered on a given poker hand up to a certain cap. The cap for smaller games is usually $4 and even for larger games generally does not exceed $10. Additionally, the sites take a fee from each online tournament held. For example, for a $500 tournament, $450 of a player's entrance fee might go into the prize pool while $50 would be kept by the online cardroom as a charge for hosting and running the tournament. Despite these modest figures, the Internet gambling industry is estimated by Business Week to be a $12 billion per year business.[30] In December 2003, it was reported that online poker revenues stood at around $34m per month and were growing by 27% per month.[31] By March 2005, during peak hours, approximately 100,000 people were playing for real money at various online cardrooms, and a similar number were playing free games.[32] Additionally, estimates put the amount gambled on internet poker sites at upwards of $60 billion for 2005.[33] Online poker sites generated revenues of approximately $200 million per month in 2005.[34]

Online poker sites are not the only entities making money from internet poker. Credit card companies, advertising agencies, and other related industries are also capturing significant profits. Additionally, internet "money transferers" such as Neteller and Firepay are also reaping profits.[35] These service providers act as intermediaries between banks/credit card companies and online poker accounts. Often, credit card companies refuse to allow credit card holders to

---

of his/her choice and the losers receive a monetary award, albeit a lesser monetary award, for the charity of their choice.
  27. Many sites also accept bank checks, see, e.g., www.partypoker.com.
  28. See below for more detail on this process.
  29. See Fuller v. Harrah's Entertainment, Inc., 2004 WL 2452771 (E.D. La. 2004).
  30. See Kerry Capell, Britain bets on Casino Games, BUSINESS WEEK ONLINE, tp://www.businessweek.com/globalbiz/content/may2006/gb20060515_495673.htm
  31. See , generally, http://en.wikipedia.org/wiki/Online_poker [hereinafter WO]
  32. Id.
  33. See Linda Johnson, More Odds and Ends, CARDPLAYER MAGAZINE VOLUME 19 NO. 4, March 7, 2006.
  34. See WO, supra WO, note 31.
  35. See, e.g. www. neteller.com; www.firepay.com

charge money to their online poker account directly from their credit cards.[36] A service such as Neteller allows users to circumvent this restriction by transferring money from either their credit cards or directly from their checking accounts to a holding account run by Neteller. The users can then transfer the funds from their Neteller account to online poker sites. The Neteller accounts also allow the inverse: one can move money from a poker site account to a Neteller account and then request that Neteller send a check. Neteller makes a profit by charging a small fee each time money is withdrawn from a Neteller account and sent back to the user. Neteller is a publicly traded company on the British stock exchange and conducted online money transfers exceeding $3.4 billion in 2004.[37]

While there are anywhere between ten and twenty online poker arenas, the six industry leaders, as of mid-2005, were partypoker.com, pokerstars.com, fulltiltpoker.com, ultimatebet.com, pokerroom.com and paradisepoker.com. Two of these sites are even publicly traded in England. PartyGaming, the parent company of PartyPoker, the largest online cardroom in 2005, went public on the London Stock Exchange, achieving an initial public offering market value in excess of $8 billion dollars. "At the time of the IPO, ninety-two percent of PartyGaming's income came from poker operations."[38] "Due to concerns about the legality of online gambling in the United States, the company is incorporated in Gibraltar and has no assets in the United States. U.S. consumers represent around 60% of PartyGaming's revenues."[39] After only 5 years of being in business, PartyGaming became the seventh largest gambling entity in the world with a market capitalization of almost $11 billion.[40] Pokerstars is the second largest online poker room. It is headquartered on the Isle of Man in the Irish Sea and is owned by Rational Enterprises, a Costa Rican company.[41]

There are several reasons why these online gambling ventures prove so profitable. First and foremost, these companies have very low overhead costs. Once the servers are set up, it takes a minimal staff to keep them running correctly. Additionally, unlike brick and mortar casinos, online casinos do not have to pay dealers, pit bosses, or other personnel. Nor do they have to pay for chips or cards. Second, online casinos can reach a significantly larger clientele than land-based casinos. For example, online poker rooms can reach residents of states that do not allow gambling and can also attract players who are under twenty-one years of age.[42] Moreover, unlike land-based casino poker rooms, which lose business on weekdays or late at night, online poker rooms never shut down; given the massive array of time zones across the globe, it is always time for poker somewhere. Furthermore, whereas brick and mortar card rooms have a fixed number of dealers and tables, online sites have a virtually unlimited number. Thus, players rarely have to wait to get seats. Third, online sites can deal more hands per hour than in brick and mortar casinos because of online dealing technology. Due to these and other delays common in brick and mortar casinos, their "average rate of play is around thirty hands per hour. Online casinos, however, do not have these delays; the dealing and shuffling are instant, there are no delays relating to counting chips, and, on average, the play is faster due to

---

[36] For example, my credit card companies. *Also see*, D Day CARDTRAK, July 2002, on http://www.cardweb.com/cardtrak/pastissues/july02.html. This article discusses how "Citibank will block transactions that are identified by transaction code as casinos and Web sites as online gambling."
[37] *See* http://about.neteller.com/aboutneteller/
[38] *See generally*, http://en.wikipedia.org/wiki/Online_poker
[39] *See* http://en.wikipedia.org/wiki/Party_Poker
[40] *See* http://finance.google.com/finance?catid=60427371 (last visited May 02, 2005)
[41] *See* http://en.wikipedia.org/wiki/Poker_Stars
[42] Most online poker sites have an 18 year old minimum, *see, e.g.*, www.pokerstars.com or www.partypoker.com.

"auto-action" buttons (which allow a player to select his action before his turn). It is not uncommon for an online poker table to average sixty to eighty hands per hour."[43]

How are these profitable businesses regulated by the United States government? In short, they are not. In order to avoid the murky question of whether it is legal to operate an online poker business on United States soil, all the major sites have chosen to incorporate in foreign jurisdictions, the most popular of which include Costa Rica, England, and Canada.[44] These countries possess the ideal qualities of lax regulation of the internet poker industry as well as having officially made the game legal.[45] The United States has chosen not to impose any regulations specifically on the online poker industry. Rather, in the Safe Port Act passed and signed into law in October of 2006, the U.S. government has attempted to ban it.[46][47] However, as will be explained in detail below, the Safe Port Act does not prevent all internet poker sites from operating. Thus, the U.S. government's decision to attempt to prohibit internet poker rather than to regulate it has and will lead to a host of legal and public policy quagmires. First, there is no governmental enforcement mechanism to monitor and regulate cheating or other illicit behavior by the operators of these sites.[48] Second, absent regulation, states lose the opportunity to enforce some of their social policies. For example, in some states, the legal gambling age is twenty-one. Online, a person need only be eighteen to gamble. In fact, teenagers have been some of the largest online money winners.[49] In addition, because gambling is often regulated on a state level, it also has state sovereignty implications. Also, by failing to get involved, the US loses some of its ability to control negative social spillovers that sometimes result from gambling, such as crime and addiction. Finally, the U.S. loses its ability to monitor the taxable income flowing between U.S. citizens and these sites and to tax these sites' profits.[50]

[43.] *See* http://en.wikipedia.org/wiki/Online_poker;

[44.] *See generally,* Mark G. Tratos, *Gaming on the Internet III: The Politics of Internet Gaming and the Genesis of Legal Bans or Licensing*, 610 PLI/PAT 711, 719–22 (2000); Seth Gorman & Antony Loo, *Black Jack or Bust: Can U.S. Law Stop Internet Gambling?*, 16 LOY. L.A. ENT. L. J. 667–9 (1996).

[45.] *See* Mike Brunker, *Australia, U.S. at Odds on Net Betting*, http://www.msnbc.com/NEWS/287419.asp (last visited January 7, 2006); Mike Brunker, *Britain Embraces Internet Gambling*, http://www.msnbc.com/news/540530.asp (last visited January, 7, 2006).

[46.] *See* CARDPLAYER MAGAZINE ONLINE (www.cardplayer.com/pokerlaw/allynshulman_testimony.pdf), "Poker and the Law section": "This content was taken from Allyn Jaffrey Shulman's testimony on HB 1509 to the North Dakota State Senate. Her testimony was entitled "Three Issues Regarding Online Poker: Legality, Congressional Efforts and Poker is a Game of Skill"": "The United States is a paradox when it comes to online poker. Estimates put the US share of the world's online poker market as high as nearly 80%. Yet this is the only market that allows the $2 billion online poker industry to operate in an unregulated environment. Without regulation, it is difficult to manage issues such as underage gambling, excessive gambling, fraud, collusion, and money laundering. The United States is moving in a direction completely opposite to the rest of the world when it comes to online poker. Rather than accept the fact that online poker is here to stay and demand safeguards to prevent underage gambling, overspending by players, and collusion during poker games, as regulators in other countries have done, the US is trying to prohibit this thriving industry." (last visited January 19, 2006).

[47] H.R. 4954 (http://www.rules.house.gov/109_2nd/text/hr4954cr/hr49543_portscr.pdf or http://www.pocketfives.com/68CBB9B1-C383-45BF-8308-13BBFE1C37BC.aspx)

[48.] Some sites are audited by Price Waterhouse Coopers or licensed by Native American Tribal Gaming boards.

[49.] *See* www.zeejustin.com; (noting that large online money winner Justin Bonomo began his gambling career at age 19.)

[50.] *See* the section entitled "The Pros and Cons of Regulating Online Poker" infra, for an in-depth analysis of these public policy issues.

This paper begins with an overview of the history of the legality of internet poker. First, it examines legal scholars' opinions of whether it is legal for <u>individuals</u> (players) to place wagers on internet poker sites. Second, it will look at government officials' previous attempts to criminalize online gambling using state and federal law. Third, it will examine the specific federal laws, namely the Wire, Travel, and Illegal Gambling Business Acts, that the government has always claimed has criminalized the operating of an online gambling business, focusing particularly on the impact of the jurisdictional reach of these laws. Fourth, it will examine the legislature's previous attempts to specifically criminalize owning and operating an internet poker website. Fifth, it will analyze the impact of the Safe Port Act on internet gambling and once again discuss the jurisdictional problems this law might run into. Next, it examines what steps, if any, the US government has taken toward regulating the online poker industry. Then, it weighs the pros and cons of regulation and also analyzes several potential regulatory constructs. Finally, it attempts to distinguish poker from other forms of gambling.

II) HISTORY OF THE LEGALITY OF ONLINE POKER

Before examining the Safe Port Act or Congress' previous attempts to criminalize the running of an online gambling business, it is important to look at the government's previous legal assertions regarding online gambling. None of the major online poker interests have ever been the target of a prosecution by the United States government. First, it is worth considering what legal scholars have to say about the legality for players participating in online gambling. Next, it is important to examine the laws government officials have previously (and still do) cited as prohibiting the running of an online gambling institution. Only after these two issues have been addressed can previous legislation and the Safe Port Act be accurately and properly analyzed.

A) LEGAL SCHOLARS' OPINIONS

Two of the nation's preeminent gambling law scholars are Professor I. Nelson Rose and Chuck Humphrey, Esq. Professor Rose is a tenured faculty member at Whittier Law School in California and author of numerous gambling law books, including his most recent work "Internet Gaming Law."[51] Mr. Humphrey is a former partner at Kirkland & Ellis, founding

---

[51]. From I. Nelson Rose's website, www.gamblingandthelaw.com : "Professor I. Nelson Rose is recognized as one of the world's leading authorities on gambling law. He is an internationally known scholar, with more than 500 published works, and public speaker, often the keynote speaker on gambling issues. A 1979 graduate of Harvard Law School, he is a tenured full Professor at Whittier Law School in Costa Mesa, California, where he teaches one of the first law school classes on gaming law. Professor Rose is best known for his internationally syndicated column, "Gambling and the Law®," and his landmark 1986 book by the same name. His most recent books are a collection of columns and analysis, co-authored with Bob Loeb, Blackjack and the Law, and the first casebook on gaming law, Gaming Law: Cases and Materials (LexisNexis/Matthew Bender 2003), co-authored with Professors Robert Jarvis, Shannon Bybee, J. Wesley Cochran and Ronald Rychlak. Professor Rose's latest book, Internet Gaming Law, co-authored with Martin Owens, has just been published by Mary Ann Liebert Publishers. A consultant to governments and industry, Professor Rose has testified as an expert witness in administrative, civil and criminal cases in the U.S., Australia and New Zealand, and has acted as a consultant to major law firms, international corporations, licensed casinos, players, Native American tribes, and local, state and national governments, including Arizona, California, Florida, Illinois, Michigan, New Jersey, Texas, the province of Ontario, and the federal governments of Canada and the United States. With the rising interest in

partner of Addoms and Humphrey, and principal investor/founder of Tournament of Champions Poker.[52] While both scholars have impressive credentials and extensive knowledge of gaming law, they have slightly differing opinions about the legality of online poker for players. Therefore, this section shall initially give a brief overview of the legality of online poker for players before it considers the legality for the companies running the online poker sites, which essentially govern the question of whether online poker can legally exist in its current form.

In his article, "Is it a Crime to Play Poker On-line?," Professor Rose considers whether it is legal for a poker player to play online. Professor Rose argues that "federal law is clear" and that "the federal government's interest in gambling is pretty much limited to organized crime."[53] Therefore, he believes that internet poker players should not fear that the federal government will issue warrants for their arrest for playing online. He comments that "a regular player cannot get into trouble with the federal government even if the gambling operation is blatantly illegal, unless he does something to help the business." He also notes that the few times the Department of Justice has charged regular players with crimes, judges dismissed the cases.[54]

Looking at state rather than federal law, Professor Rose writes that "all states make it a crime to conduct some forms of unauthorized gambling. But about half the states also make it a crime to make a bet under some circumstances, even though nobody is ever charged any more." Using California as an example, Professor Rose notes that California Penal Code Sec. 330 provides: "Every person who plays . . . any banking or percentage game played with cards . . . for money, checks, credit, or other representative of value, and every person who plays or bets at or against any of those prohibited games, is guilty of a misdemeanor . . . ." Professor Rose concludes that in California "it seems it is not a crime to play poker online for money, if the game is not a percentage game."[55]

In his article, "Is Playing Poker Online in California Legal?," Chuck Humphrey refutes some of Professor Rose's contentions. Specifically, he regards playing online poker as a percentage game because of the rake. Therefore, he concludes that it is illegal for a person to play poker online in California.[56] Thus, in Mr. Humphrey's view, "the better, more legally

---

gambling throughout the world, Professor Rose has been invited as a public speaker to address such diverse groups as the National Conference of State Legislatures, Congress of State Lotteries of Europe, United States Conference of Mayors, and the National Academy of Sciences. He has taught classes on gaming law to the F.B.I., at the University of Ljubljana in Slovenia and as a Visiting Scholar for the University of Nevada-Reno's Institute for the Study of Gambling and Commercial Gaming. Prof. Rose has presented scholarly papers on gambling in Nevada, New Jersey, Puerto Rico, England, Australia, Antigua, Portugal, Italy, Argentina and the Czech Republic."

[52.] From Mr. Humphrey's website, www.gambling-law-us.com: "Chuck Humphrey began practicing law in 1968. He was a partner in the national firm of Kirkland & Ellis when, in 1986, he became one of the two founding partners of Addoms & Humphrey, a Business Development Company that assisted in structuring and financing new ventures. In 1999 he became the principal investor in and one of the founders of the Tournament of Champions of Poker and of Team Pegasus, an association of professional tournament poker players. He is admitted to practice law in Colorado, Michigan and Texas, currently being active in Colorado, where he lives. He was a staff attorney for the Securities and Exchange Commission in Washington, D.C. early in his legal career. Chuck continues his law practice, which principally focuses on business matters, including gambling law, structuring transactions, and securities and venture capital law."

[53.] I. Nelson Rose, *Is It a Crime to Play Online?*, 7 GAMLR 409, 410 (December, 2003).
[54.] *Id.*
[55.] *Id.*
[56.] *See* Charles Humphrey, Esq., *Is it a Crime to Play Online Poker in California?*, http://www.gambling-law-us.com/Articles-Notes/play-online-california.htm. Mr. Humphrey] believe[s]

supportable conclusion is: playing poker for money in California at the popular online poker websites is illegal, but in today's tolerant atmosphere the risk of being charged with a criminal misdemeanor is far less than the chance of getting a speeding ticket, and the actual penalty to befall anyone who is charged will be not much more serious than the speeding ticket."[57] He ends the article by quoting Professor Rose who states, "Half the states do have ancient laws on the book making it illegal to make a bet. But, probably 20 million Americans make technically forbidden wagers each year. With odds like that, you are more likely to be elected governor of California than charged with illegal gambling."[58]

So Professor Rose and Mr. Humphrey seem to agree in principle that it is possible that antiquated state laws to make it illegal for a player to play poker online. However, both scholars agree that the probability or consequences of a prosecution are minimal.

The only state to explicitly outlaw internet gambling is Washington.[59] In May 2006, the Washington State Legislature passed Senate Bill 6613, which makes it a class C felony for a person situated in Washington to place a wager over the internet.[60] However, this bill will be hard to enforce. First, there is no agency set up to enforce this law. Second, it will be very difficult, if not impossible, to target individuals who are engaged in the prohibited wagering—short of placing a tracing device in a person's computer, or monitoring an individual's credit card, it would be hard to ascertain these persons' identities. The only official action the Washington state government has taken regarding this legislation is to threaten publications such as the Seattle Times for linking to poker websites.[61]

Given (1) the fact that it isn't illegal for an individual to play online poker under federal law, (2) the lack of enforcement of these state laws against internet gamblers, and (3) general confusion about whether state courts have the jurisdiction to apply these laws, the question of whether it is illegal under a given state's laws for an individual to play internet poker is virtually moot. The more interesting question is whether it is illegal to own, operate, or otherwise participate in an online poker business.

---

the existence of the rake or entry fee makes the poker game a percentage game, all of which are banned as a class by Section 330. *Sullivan v. Fox*, 189 Cal.App.3d 673, 235 Cal.Rptr. 5 (Cal.App. 1 Dist., 1987) provided the first stated "interpretation of what constitutes a percentage game under California law... Three different methods of calculating the amounts to be paid to the house by players were considered: (1) a portion of each participants winnings, (2) a fixed portion of the amount of each bet, or (3) the time that each participant plays. The court held that if either of the first two methods is used, then the game will be a percentage game."

[57] *See id.*
[58] *Id.* quoting I. Nelson Rose, *Guilty of Gambling Online?*, CARD PLAYER MAGAZINE Vol. 16, Mo. 21, Oct. 10, 2003.
[59] *See* Earl Burton, *Washington State Passes Online Poker and Gaming Legislation*, POKERNEWS, (http://www.pokernews.com/news/2006/5/washington-state-online-poker-legislation.htm)
[60] Wash. SB 6613
[61] *See* Danny Westneat, *This Column May Be Illegal*, SEATTLE TIMES, (http://seattletimes.nwsource.com/html/localnews/2003062386_danny15.html) and http://www.neverwinpoker.com/phpnuke/html/article-498-thread-1-0.html

B) GOVERNMENT OFFICIALS' ACTIONS/OPINIONS

Several states have gambling laws that could be construed to make the running of an online poker business illegal.[62] However, very few prosecutions have been undertaken, and those usually have been undertaken by the US Attorney's Office rather than by state law enforcement officials. The most noteworthy instance of prosecution of a participant in online gambling occurred in *United States v. Cohen*.[63]

In 1998, the U.S. Attorney for New York filed charges against fourteen individuals connected with six separate internet sports books.[64] Several defendants took plea bargains, but Jay Cohen, a former San Francisco options trader, took his case to trial, marking the first ever federal prosecution for internet gambling.[65] The US Attorney charged Cohen with conspiracy to violate the Wire Act (18 USC 1084). Cohen founded World Sports Exchange (WSE) in Antigua. WSE's only purpose was to take bets on sporting events over the internet.[66] A jury found Cohen guilty of conspiracy and the Second Circuit upheld his conviction holding that his belief that his actions were legal and the fact that his business was licensed in Antigua did not constitute cause to overturn his conviction.[67]

Despite the 2nd Circuit's ruling, there are several important reasons why neither this case, nor the cases that resulted in plea agreements, shed much light on the legality of internet poker. First, poker was not at issue in these cases. In fact, casino gambling itself was not at issue. WSE conducted only a sports gambling operation, which is clearly under the purview of the Wire Act. Second, only Americans were charged, avoiding the ambiguous question of whether foreign nationals or foreign companies could be charged. Third, unlike the internet poker sites, these internet sports books "each took at least one bet over the telephone, giving prosecutors a fall-back position if a court rules the Wire Act does not apply to the Internet." Fourth, and most importantly, unlike any of the internet poker businesses, these sports betting companies had significant ties to the United States: the defendants sent mail within the U.S., the companies had U.S. 1–800 numbers, the defendants wrote business checks from U.S. banks, etc. As previously mentioned, internet poker sites generally go out of their way to have absolutely no ties to the United States whatsoever.[68] A criminal complaint has yet to be filed against a purely foreign corporation or a foreign national and no complaint has ever been filed against a company running an internet card room.

In addition to undertaking these peripherally applicable prosecutions, several prominent government officials took it upon themselves to weigh in on the question of whether or not internet poker is legal under laws existing before the passage of the Safe Port Act. The most significant example of this occurred in late 2003 when Assistant Attorney General John G. Malcolm sent a letter (the "Malcolm Letter") to the National Association of Broadcasters, "encouraging" them not to accept advertising from online gambling sites. Malcolm's letter reads in relevant part: "The sheer volume of advertisements [relating to internet gambling] . . . is

---

[62] *See generally*, Charles Humphrey, Esq., *State Gambling Law Summary*, http://www.gambling-law-us.com/State-Law-Summary/.
[63] United States v. Cohen, 260 F.3d 68 (2d Cir. 2001).
[64] *See* I. Nelson Rose, *The Law of Internet Gambling*, GAMBLING AND THE LAW, http://www.gamblingandthelaw.com/internet.html [hereinafter GL].
[65] Technically, 14 defendants were named in separate criminal complaints, but Cohen was the only one to go to trial.
[66] *See* GL, *supra* note 64.
[67] Cohen, *supra* note 63 at 73.
[68] *See generally* GL, *supra* note 64.

troubling because it misleads the public in the United States into believing that such gambling activity is legal, when, in fact, it is not. Because of the possibility that some of your organization's members may be accepting money to place such advertisements, the Department of Justice, as a public service, would like you to be aware that the entities and individuals placing these advertisements MAY be violating various state and federal laws and that the entities and individuals that accept and run such advertisements MAY be aiding and abetting these illegal activities." (emphasis added)[69] The letter goes on to state: "Notwithstanding their frequent claims of legitimacy, Internet gambling . . operations that accept bets from customers in the United States violate Sections 1084, [70] 1952, and 1055 of Title 18 of the United States Code."[71]

III) EXISTING LAW

This section examines the federal laws that the government referenced as criminalizing internet poker prior to the passage of the Safe Port Act. It then considers the impact of state law. Next, it discusses whether the government, in bringing an action against an internet gambling company, can acquire jurisdiction over the company in general. Finally, it considers the particularly complex issues involved in gaining jurisdiction over a purely foreign corporation, such as PartyGaming or PokerStars, whose only contacts in the United States come via internet communication. It is particularly important for the reader to read and consider the analyses of the various laws and jurisdictional issues together, as they are inherently intertwined. Furthermore, different jurisdictional analyses will apply to different laws, e.g. state/civil, state/criminal, federal/civil, federal/criminal, which necessitates reading the sections as a whole for proper understanding.

Additionally, on occasion various laws affect poker differently than other forms of gambling. Different laws may treat all types of gambling as the same or split it into any combination of three categories: 1) table games such as blackjack, roulette, and other games of chance, 2) skill/semi-skill games, and 3) sports wagering.[72] Enough variations exist for the subject of a whole other article. In general, the laws discussed below, while couched in terms of general gambling, encompass poker as well.[73]

---

[69] For content of the letter and comments on Assistant Attorney General Malcolm's motives *see* Allyn Jaffrey Shulman, *Turning Up the Heat*, CARDPLAYER ONLINE NEWSLETTER, October 29, 2003 (http://www.cardplayer.com/poker_magazine/archives/?a_id=13636&m_id=7). Emphasis was added by Ms. Shulman, not I.

[70] *Id.*

[71] Please see generous discussion of Sections 1084, 1952, and 1055 of Title 18 of the United States Code (The Wire Act, the Travel Act, and the Illegal Gambling Business Act, respectively) which appears below in the "Existing Law" section.

[72] Several states that disallow table games allow for public card rooms where poker may be played. Also, some states allow for slot machines to exist but not table games. *See* http://www.gambling-law-us.com/State-Laws/ for a break down of each states laws.

[73] It will be my contention that, in addition to the fact that the government should either regulate or deem illegal online poker, poker is a game of skill (thus negating some of its social ills and increasing its legitimacy) and as such should be treated differently by the law. *See* the "Conclusion" Section.

A) FEDERAL LAW

The three main laws cited by legal scholars and government officials as criminalizing online gambling prior to the Safe Port Act are the Wire Act[74], the Travel Act[75], and the Illegal Gambling Business Act[76].

B) THE WIRE ACT (18 USC §1084)

The Wire Act prohibits anyone "engaged in the business of betting or wagering" from "knowingly use[ing] a wire communication facility for the transmission in interstate or foreign commerce of bets or wagers or information assisting in the placing of bets or wagers on any sporting event or contest."[77] Upon first reading, as the authors of one of the first articles on online gambling did, it is reasonable to conclude that the Wire Act applies to online poker.[78] However, it depends on whether the clauses above are read separately or jointly. Read separately, the act prohibits ANY bets or wagers that are transmitted interstate.[79] Read jointly, the Wire Act only prohibits bets or wagers on a sporting event or contest.[80] Several experts believe that it was Congress's intent for the Wire Act to be targeted only at bookmakers and therefore should only apply to sports wagers.[81]

More telling is the court's opinion in *In Re MasterCard Intern. Inc., Internet Gambling Litigation*.[82] In *In Re Mastercard*, the court held that the plain language of the Wire Act applied only to sporting events.[83] In reaching this determination the court looked at the legislative history of the law and also the fact that recent "legislative attempts have sought to amend the Wire Act to encompass "contest[s] of chance or a future contingent event not under the control or influence of [the bettor]."[84] The Fifth Circuit affirmed the District Court's holding, stating "The district court concluded that the Wire Act concerns gambling on sporting events or contests and that the Plaintiffs had failed to allege that they had engaged in internet sports gambling. We agree with the district court's statutory interpretation, its reading of the relevant case law, its summary of the relevant legislative history, and its conclusion."[85] While the Department of Justice continues to maintain that the Wire Act criminalized all forms of online gambling, based on the *Mastercard* decision, it seems unlikely that its theory will prevail in court.

---

[74] 18 USC § 1084.
[75] 18 USC § 1952.
[76] 18 USC § 1955.
[77] The Wire Act, 18 USC § 1084.
[78] Seth Gorman & Antony Loo, *Black Jack or Bust: Can U.S. Law Stop Internet Gambling?*, 16 LOY. L.A. ENT. L. J. 667–9 (1996). "One statute that applies to Internet gambling is the Wire Act;" "This statute clearly applies to Internet casinos; however, it does not seem to apply to access providers and players."
[79] Namely "any bet or wager"—on sports events, on roulette, on poker, on anything.
[80] Just wagers relating to "sporting events or contests."
[81] *See*, *e.g.*, Jeffrey Rodefer, *Federal Wire Wager Act*, http://www.gambling-law-us.com/Federal-Laws/wire-act.htm and Allyn Jaffrey Shulman, *Turning Up the Heat*, CARDPLAYER ONLINE NEWSLETTER, October 29, 2003, http://www.cardplayer.com/poker_magazine/archives/?a_id=13636&m_id=74.
[82] 132 F.Supp.2d 468 (E.D. La. 2001).
[83] *Id.* at 480.
[84] *Id.*
[85] In Re MasterCard Intern, Inc., 313 F.3d 257, 262–3 (5th Cir. 2002).

C) THE TRAVEL ACT (18 USC §1952)

The Travel Act, in relevant part, prohibits traveling in interstate commerce or using the "mail or any facility" to "promote, manage, establish, carry on, or facilitate the promotion, management, establishment, or carrying on, of any unlawful activity."[86] This statute defines an "unlawful activity" for its purposes as "any business enterprise involving gambling . . ." and other activities normally associated with racketeering.[87] Congress passed this act around the same time as the Wire Act; both were part of President John F. Kennedy's attempt to squelch organized crime and racketeering.[88]

Essentially, the government must show two things to convict an online poker room operator of violating the Travel Act. First, the government must show that the operator violated a gambling law. Since gambling itself is regulated solely by the states, the government must demonstrate a violation of a specific state's[89] anti-gambling laws.[90] Second, the government must prove that the operator used the "mail or any facility" in furtherance of illegal gambling. The court has held that a "facility" for the purpose of interstate commerce can include "use of the mail, telephone or telegraph, newspapers, credit cards and tickertapes."[91] The court is likely to find that the internet is a facility as well, either because the internet utilizes phone lines or simply by analogy.[92]

It seems clear based on the plain text of this law that as long as the government can show a violation of a state anti-gambling law, then a conviction under the Travel Act should follow.

D) THE ILLEGAL GAMBLING BUSINESS ACT (18 USC §1955)

The Illegal Gambling Business Act states that "whoever conducts, finances, manages, supervises, directs, or owns all or part of an illegal gambling business" shall be fined or imprisoned.[93] This statute defines an "illegal gambling business" as, among other things, a gambling business which "is a violation of the law of a State."[94] Although Congress passed this

---

[86] 18 U.S.C. § 1952.

[87] Id.

[88] See Jeffrey Rodefer, Federal Travel Act Scopes and Predicates, http://www.gambling-law-us.com/Federal-Laws/travel-act.htm : "As part of United States Attorney General Robert F. Kennedy's program to combat organized crime and racketeering, Congress enacted the Travel Act in 1961 as part of the same series of legislation as the Wire Act."

[89] See Chuck Humphrey, Application of Federal Anti-Gambling Laws to Internet Cardrooms: "The question is not whether the player is violating the law, but rather whether the operation of the online cardroom violates applicable state laws that criminalize the operation of professional gambling facilities."

[90] Id. "It is important to note that the Travel Act "refers to state law only to identify the defendant's unlawful activity, the federal crime to be proved in § 1952 is use of the interstate facilities in furtherance of the unlawful activity, not the violation of state law; therefore § 1952 does not require that the state crime ever be completed." Citing: United States v. Campione, 942 F.2d 429, 434 (7th Cir. 1991).

[91] See Jeffrey Rodefer, Federal Travel Act Scopes and Predicates, http://www.gambling-law-us.com/Federal-Laws/travel-act.htm.

[92] The court in U.S. v. Smith, 209 F. Supp. 907 (E.D. Ill. 1962), noted that "because telephone voices are "actually transported by wires across state lines to the same extent as materials are transported over state lines in moving vehicles," the Travel Act encompasses acts transmitted over telephone rather than only acts of actual physical travel. The same can be said of acts committed over the internet.

[93] 18 USC § 1955.

[94] Id. at (b)(1)(i).

statute with organized crime in mind, [95] it seems applicable to internet gambling operators as well.[96] The government must simply show that the operator runs a business that involves gambling that is contrary to a state law. [97] As Mr. Humphrey puts it, "Gambling Web sites are subject to the same regulatory and licensing requirements as the off-line world. What is illegal off-line remains illegal online; it is illegal to offer (Internet) gambling services to consumers resident in a country where a license has not been granted by the appropriate authorities."[98] However, again, the question of whether an internet poker room operator has violated the Illegal Gambling Business Act turns on an inquiry into the particular state law that he is accused of violating.

E) STATE LAW

Based on the previous discussion, it seems that the Wire Act would not apply to internet poker operators, but the Travel Act and the Illegal Gambling Business Act would as long as the operators violated a specific state's anti-gambling laws. Of course, the state would also be able to prosecute these operators for violation of those same state laws.

Every state has anti-gambling laws that may do a variety of things: prohibit gambling outright, prohibit certain types of gambling, prohibit running a gambling establishment without a license, etc. Some states make exceptions and allow card rooms to operate as long as they have a state license and do not allow any other type of gambling on the premises. However, it is safe to say that operating a poker room or establishment that charges a rake violates at least one anti-gambling law in over two-thirds of the states. In fact, Mr. Humphrey writes that "the offering and conduct of online gambling activities probably violates the criminal laws of every state in the United States."

Therefore, it is probable that internet pokerroom operators are guilty of violating not only these state laws, but also the Travel Act and Illegal Gambling Business Act. However, all internet poker sites are run completely offshore. Traditionally, the applicable law is that of the state (or the country) where the bet takes place; the "correct test is whether the gambling offered by the online casino would be legal if it were conducted in person in the place where the bettor is located." Thus, since at least part of the crime in question takes place in the United States, the government can likely charge internet pokerroom operators with violations of state law, the Travel Act, and the Illegal Gambling Business Act. However, in order to proceed successfully with a prosecution, the government also must have jurisdiction over these operators.

[95.] *See* United States v. Sacco, 491 F.2d 995, 998 (9th Cir. 1974).

[96.] Seth Gorman & Antony Loo, *Black Jack or Bust: Can U.S. Law Stop Internet Gambling?*, 16 LOY. L.A. ENT. L. J. 667–9 (1996) and Jeffrey Rodefer, *Illegal Gambling Business Act of 1970*, http://www.gambling-law-us.com/Federal-Laws/illegal-gambling.htm.

[97.] An important note: I am discussing only the most important and relevant parts of these federal laws. The government must also prove other things to secure convictions under the 3 laws discussed. For example, to violate the Illegal Gambling Business Act, the business in question must involve 5 or more people and run for more than 30 days. The parts not discussed are fairly straight forward and one can assume that the government can prove the portions against internet gambling operators without much difficulty.

[98.] *See* Humphrey, *supra* note 89.

IV) JURISDICTIONAL ISSUES

Civil suits by the government against a foreign/out-of-state corporation have been around for centuries. Personal jurisdiction over an out-of-state corporation is proper if it is both authorized by statute and does not violate the Due Process Clause of the Fourteenth Amendment.[99] This section shall assume that each state has enacted an appropriate long-arm statute to satisfy the first prong. For the second prong, the standard test articulated in *International Shoe* and its progeny has been used for over six decades.[100] Due Process requires that the defendant have "minimum contacts"[101] with the forum state and also that the jurisdiction does not offend "traditional notions of fair play and substantial justice.[102] The court has expanded and contracted the requirements for "minimum contacts" throughout the years. A court may gain specific personal jurisdiction over a defendant if he has sufficient minimum contacts with the forum relating to the facts underlying the pending case (in this case, a civil case against a corporation for violating gambling law over the internet)[103] or if the defendant purposely directed his activities toward the forum state.[104]

The internet has severely complicated this analysis. In the case of internet gambling companies, their actions clearly affect people in a given state, but that corporation never sets foot in that state nor does it specifically send any material to that state. The question is whether the establishment of a gambling website which is created by a foreign corporation and sent over out-of-state (or country) servers into a given state constitutes enough contact to establish jurisdiction over the corporation.

Given that this is a relatively novel question, the Circuit Courts of the United States have yet to speak on it. However, several districts Courts have adopted the standard outlined in *Zippo Mfg Co. v. Zippo Dot Com, Inc.*[105] *Zippo* articulates a "sliding-scale" test that evaluates "the nature and quality of activity that a defendant conducts over the Internet."[106] At one end of the scale "lie businesses or persons who clearly conduct business over the Internet and have repeated contacts with the forum state."[107] In such instances, jurisdiction is clearly proper. On the other side of this continuum lie passive websites. A passive website "does little more than make information available to those who are interested in it [and] is not grounds for the exercise of personal jurisdiction."[108] The middle of this continuum "is occupied by interactive Web sites where a user can exchange information with the host computer," and, there, "the exercise of

---

[99] Burnham v. Superior Court of California, County of Marin, 495 U.S. 604, 609 (1990); Asahi Metal Industry Co., Ltd. v. Superior Court of California, Solano County, 480 U.S. 102, 107; Burger King Corp. v. Rudzewicz, 471 U.S. 462 (1985); World-Wide Volkswagen Corp. v. Woodson, 444 U.S. 286 (1980); Hanson v. Denckla, 357 U.S. 235 (1958); International Shoe Co. v. State of Wash., Office of Unemployment Compensation and Placement, 326 U.S. 310 (1945).

[100] 326 U.S. 310 (1945).

[101] *See* World-Wide Volkswagon v. Woodson, 444 U.S. 286, 297 (1980).

[102] *Id.*

[103] Helicopteros Nacionales de Colombia, S.A. v. Hall, 466 U.S. 408 (1984).

[104] Burger King, 471 U.S. 462, 472 (1985); Calder v. Jones, 465 U.S. 783 (1984); Keeton v. Hustler Magazine, Inc., 465 U.S. 770, 774 (1984).

[105] 952 F.Supp. 1119, 1120 (W.D. Pa. 1997).

[106] *Id.* at 1123.

[107] *See* Alitalia-Linee Aeree Italiane S.p.A. v. Casinoalitalia.Com, 128 F.Supp.2d 340, 349 (E.D.Va. 2001).

[108] *See* Zippo, 952 F.Supp. 1119, at 1124.

jurisdiction is determined by examining the level of interactivity and commercial nature of the exchange of information that occurs on the Web site."[109]

Internet poker websites fall within this middle ground. Upon examining the level of interactivity of a poker website, one would clearly conclude that it rises to a sufficient level to justify jurisdiction under the *Zippo* standard. A poker website "provides intense real-time interactivity to its members," as members need to download a program, place money onto the site, and access the site each time they want to play.[110] In fact, "online casino gambling is an inherently interactive activity."[111] This was the exact conclusion of the court in *Alitalia-Linee Aeree Italiane S.p.A. v. Casinoalitalia.Com.*[112] In *Alitalia*, the plaintiff, an Italian airline, sued Casinoalitalia.Com for a trademark violation. The defendant was an internet casino operator established under the laws of the Dominican Republic with its headquarters in Santo Domingo. It conducted its business solely outside the United States and has no offices or personnel within U.S. borders. Nonetheless, the court found that because a gambling website is highly interactive in nature, the company intentionally availed itself of the forum and jurisdiction was therefore proper.[113] Likewise, in *Thompson v. Handa-Lopez, Inc.*, the court found personal jurisdiction over a company that runs an internet casino because of the interactive nature of the online casino.[114] In *Thompson*, an online player sued an online casino to recover winnings that the casino allegedly did not pay out. The defendant argued that personal jurisdiction did not exist because the internet casino was a California corporation with no relevant contact in Texas. The court, applying the *Zippo* standard, found "sufficient contacts with the forum state to justify the exercise of in personam jurisdiction because (i) the defendant "continuously interacted with casino players [by] entering into contracts with them as they played with various games"; (ii) the defendant "entered into contracts with the residents of various states knowing that it would receive commercial gain at the present time"; (iii) the plaintiff "played the casino games while in Texas, as if they were physically located in Texas"; and (iv) the defendant would have sent any money won to the plaintiff's Texas address."[115]

The same analysis used in *Alitalia* and *Thompson* would apply if an internet poker website was sued. A poker website is interactive. A user must download the program, the program continuously interacts with the players as the poker game occurs, and more importantly, as the courts failed to comment on, when a player deposited money into his online poker account, he had to create a profile indicating what state he was in, thus telling the site operators what state their business is going into.[116] It is clear that based on the *Zippo* standard,

---

[109] *Id.*
[110] *See* Alitalia, 128 F.Supp.2d, at 350.
[111] *Id.*
[112] *Id.*
[113] *See id.* The court avoided the problem of how, aside form establishing jurisdiction, they could proceed against a completely foreign corporation by allowing the plaintiff, as per the applicable statute, to proceed in rem against the internet casino's domain name. This particular method would not work with an internet poker site, but this does not change the jurisdictional analysis.
[114] Thompson v. Handa-Lopez, Inc, 998 F.Supp. 738 (W.D. Tex., 1998).
[115] *Id.* at 744.
[116] ALR (59 AMJUR POF 3d 1) delineated some factors which should be examined in determining whether the defendant corporation established an "internet presence" in the forum state. Those factors include: "Location of Internet Service Provider, Accessibility of website within forum, Lack of location-sensitive gateway to website that would bar forum residents from access, Number of website hits from forum residents, Leaving "cookie" on computers within forum, Maintenance of a listserv accessible within the forum, Number of listserv participants within the forum, Administration, operation or moderation of a newsgroup accessible within the forum, Posting messages to a newsgroup accessible within the forum,

a court would find personal jurisdiction to be proper over any of the major internet poker companies.

More relevant to internet poker operators is the criminal jurisdiction which our government might be able to exercise over these corporations. A corporation can rarely be held criminally liable, and based on the laws mentioned above; severe criminal penalties are not applicable to companies that run internet poker sites. However, their officers may be held accountable, such as in the case of Jay Cohen infra. In general, in criminal cases "courts have no trouble finding jurisdiction over a defendant who has caused harm within their borders."[117] The question becomes more complicated when the action in question is legal in one state but illegal in another. For example, when the internet gambling operation is situated in Nevada where gambling is legal and it is used by a person in Utah where gambling is expressly prohibited, does Utah have jurisdiction?

Nelson Rose, in his book <u>Internet Gaming Law</u>, [118] notes that there is a "strong presumption against extraterritorial application of U.S. state statutes outside the state borders."[119] In general, state A cannot convict a person who, while physically located in state B, affected state A through his internet actions. The one instance in which state A could convict this man is if state A was employing a statute that specifically contained a statement of legislative intent that the statute apply extraterritorially.[120] For example, Nevada enacted a law which expressly makes it a crime in Nevada for a person located anywhere to accept a wager over the Internet from a person physically located in Nevada.[121] Either way, this point is generally moot, given that the most applicable laws are federal, and thus, they apply in every state. Furthermore, as mentioned above, the activity in question is not legal in any state, but only in foreign jurisdictions such as Antigua; so this is likely a doubly moot point.

A) JURISDICTION OVER PURELY FOREIGN CORPORATIONS

As previously mentioned, the only cases in which the U.S. has actually exerted jurisdiction over an internet gaming company or its officers, namely Cohen and WIGC, have occurred because the companies either stipulated to jurisdiction or actually conducted part of their business on American soil. As established in the previous section, it is likely that the U.S. government can satisfy the requirements of personal jurisdiction, either in a civil or criminal capacity, over an internet defendant. The question remains, however, whether the fact that internet poker companies have no ties to the United States changes this analysis. Can the

---

Number of forum residents accessing or contributing to defendant's newsgroup, Hyperlinking a Website to other Websites active within the forum, Participating in Internet chat with forum residents, Remotely operating computers within the forum, Effecting sales via the Internet to forum residents, Transmitting products or services (such as data or programming) over the Internet to forum residents, Accepting or processing payments via the Internet, and Populating the Website with forum-related content."

[117] I. NELSON ROSE AND MARTIN D. OWENS, INTERNET GAMING LAW, (2005), at 112.

[118] *Id.* at 113.

[119] *Id.* Rose notes that the Supreme Court agrees in Neilsen v. the State of Oregon, 212 U.S. 315 (1909); The Defendant "was within the limits of the state of Washington, doing an act which that State in terms authorized and gave him license to do. Can the State of Oregon, by virtue of its concurrent jurisdiction, disregard that authority, practically override the legislation of Washington, and punish a man for doing within the territorial limits of Washington an act which that State had specifically authorized him to do? We are of opinion that it cannot."

[120] *Id.* at 114.

[121] *Id.* at 115 quoting S.B. 318 (1997), codified at NEV. REV. STAT. §§ 465.091 to 465.094.

United States extend its jurisdictional reach into Costa Rica, where PokerStars is incorporated, or to England, where PartyPoker is incorporated?

In one of the first articles to address the burgeoning question of the legality of online gaming, <u>Blackjack or Bust</u>, the authors comment, "it is clear that Congress has the power to pass legislation that regulates extraterritorial conduct."[122] They remark that the United States has enforced its laws beyond its borders since 1818.[123] While this may be true, it remains to be seen exactly how the United States is going to extend its reach into Costa Rica or other foreign countries to punish influential corporate officers. Furthermore, the authors remark that either the express language of the law applied or the clear congressional intent behind the law must indicate that it is meant to be applied extraterritorially.[124] A strong presumption against the extraterritorial application of federal criminal statute has been part of American law for decades.[125] The applicable anti-gambling laws discussed above lack the clear indication of extraterritorial intent necessary for them to apply to foreign operators. Even if they did, as noted by the authors of <u>Blackjack or Bust</u>, foreign countries will generally not aid in the enforcement of laws that conflict with the protection that they afford their corporations.[126] For example, if gambling is legal in Antigua, Antigua will likely not aid the U.S. in enforcing an anti-gambling statute against an Antiguan internet gambling company and its officers.

Assuming that a U.S. court did in fact rule that one of the anti-gambling laws applied to internet gambling, the court had personal jurisdiction over the company based on minimum contacts, and also that Congress had intended the law to apply extraterritorially, the U.S. would still have to find a way to either get the foreign corporation into U.S. court or to enforce a default judgment against that company. Professor Rose notes that there are three main methods by which the operator of an online gaming company may be brought under U.S. jurisdiction from a foreign country.[127]

First, the operator could voluntarily submit to jurisdiction. This is unlikely to happen in the case of internet poker companies. Second, by way of international treaty, the host nation can act on behalf of the United States, allowing service of process, discovery, and eventually extradition.[128]

The United States "must ensure that process is served according to applicable treaties and the enforcing country's internal laws."[129] This means if the defendant company's conduct does not violate the law of the countries where the corporation operates, such as is the case with most internet gambling companies, the foreign country is unlikely to extradite. The Hague Convention, the most widely referenced extraterritorial treaty, "an international equivalent to the United States' Full Faith and Credit Clause, binds courts of member nations to recognize one

---

[122]. Seth Gorman & Antony Loo, *Black Jack or Bust: Can U.S. Law Stop Internet Gambling?*, 16 LOY. L.A. ENT. L. J. 667–9 (1996).

[123]. *Id.*

[124]. *Id.*: "The first step in determining whether United States laws apply extraterritorially is to look at the express language of the law and the congressional intent."

[125]. *See* Professor I. Nelson Rose, *Understanding the Law of Internet Gambling*, http://www.gamblingandthelaw.com/internet_gambling.html. "This strong presumption against extraterritorial application of federal criminal statutes has been part of American law for decades."

[126]. *See* Gorman & Loo, *supra* note 127.

[127]. I. NELSON ROSE AND MARTIN D. OWENS, INTERNET GAMING LAW, (2005) at 185.

[128]. *See generally id.* at 186.

[129]. Yvonne A. Tamayo, *Catch Me if You Can: Serving United States Process on an Elusive Defendant Abroad*, 17 HARV. J. LAW. & TECH. 211.

another's judicial decisions."[130] Fifty countries are members of the Hague Convention.[131] However, in general, internet poker companies are not located in these countries. Furthermore, many of the Hague signatories claimed extensive reservations to the treaty.[132] Additionally, "much depends on the host country's willingness to cooperate."[133] The combination of these factors makes it unlikely that the U.S. can gain jurisdiction over an internet poker company located in Europe, and even more unlikely that they could gain jurisdiction over a company located in Central American or the Caribbean, where most internet poker corporations are located. Moreover, these treaties usually exist with respect to civil law; it would be near impossible for the United States to get a foreign country to agree to extradite the officers of a corporation who are operating a legal gambling business under the laws of the other country to the U.S. to face criminal charges.

The third method Professor Rose indicates may be used by the U.S. to bring a gambling site into court is to simply assert unilateral jurisdiction.[134] He notes that this is an "extraordinary and unusual process" only justified "when no lesser recourse is available."[135] In *Graduate Management Admission Council (GMAC) v. Raju*, the court found jurisdiction over a foreign website operator and citizen of India.[136] Using the *Zippo* analysis, the court found personal jurisdiction over the defendant noting that "to find otherwise would not only frustrate GMAC's attempts in this case to vindicate its rights under United States law, by requiring GMAC to turn to foreign courts to vindicate those rights against a likely elusive defendant, it would also provide a blueprint whereby other individuals bent on violating United States trademark and copyright laws could do so without risking suit in a United States court."[137] While in this case the court chose to exercise jurisdiction unilaterally, it is a rare event. The judge also entered a default judgment against Raju as he did not show up in the country for the hearing. Even in the unlikely event that the U.S. took similarly drastic action against an internet gambling site, it would be near impossible to enforce a default judgment given the location of the companies. Moreover, this sort of jurisdiction would not be utilized in a criminal case.

Foreign countries' animosity toward U.S. policy on internet gambling is further highlighted by the fact that the Caribbean nations of Antigua and Barbuda brought a case against the United States in front of the World Trade Organization claiming that U.S. laws prohibiting internet gambling violate international trade treaties signed between the countries.[138] The WTO court found that the United States violated the General Agreement of Trade in Services (GATS). The GATS requires that a country "extend the same treatment to the

---

[130] *Id.*

[131] *Id.* "Signatories to the Hague Convention are: Antigua and Barbuda, Argentina, Bahamas, Barbados, Belarus, Belgium, Botswana, Bulgaria, Canada, China, Cyprus, Czech Republic, Denmark, Egypt, Estonia, Finland, France, Germany, Greece, Ireland, Israel, Italy, Japan, Korea, Kuwait, Latvia, Lithuania, Luxembourg, Malawi, Mexico, Netherlands, Norway, Pakistan, Poland, Portugal, Russian Federation, San Marino, Seychelles, Slovak Republic, Slovenia, Spain, Sri Lanka, Sweden, Switzerland, Turkey, Ukraine, United Kingdom, United States, and Venezuela. MARTINDALE-HUBBELL, Selected International Conventions, in MARTINDALE-HUBBELL INTERNATIONAL LAW DIGEST 2003 IC-2."

[132] I. NELSON ROSE AND MARTIN D. OWENS, INTERNET GAMING LAW, (2005) at 187.

[133] *Id.*

[134] *Id.* at 189.

[135] *Id.*

[136] 241 F. Supp.2d 589 (E.D. Va., 2003).

[137] *Id.* at 600.

[138] World Trade Organization, Report of the Appellate Body: United States—Measures Affecting the Cross-Border Supply of Gambling and Betting Services; WT/DS285/AB/R, April 7, 2005. [hereinafter WTOR]

services and suppliers of any other Member that it would give its own native suppliers."[139] More important than the fact that the WTO court held that the U.S. anti-gambling laws as applied to the internet violated the GATS, is the fact that this case illustrates the fact that foreign nations are hostile toward U.S. policy on internet gambling and therefore are not to be expected to help with extradition or jurisdiction.

Simply put, the U.S. government will not be able to obtain jurisdiction over internet poker companies based offshore. One proposed alternative to prosecution of these companies is to hold the Internet Services Providers ("ISPs") accountable.[140] Access providers have a physical presence in the U.S. and also advertise within the countries borders, thus satisfying the requirements for personal jurisdiction.[141] Access providers may fold under the pressure of a threatened prosecution and simply block access to gambling websites in the U.S. This may well be why the recently proposed legislation has targeted ISPs and/or credit card companies rather than the corporations that run the internet gambling websites.

V) LEGISLATION

Before examining the Safe Port Act in detail, it is important to review the history of Congress's previous attempts to ban online gambling and to track the evolution of both the legislation itself, and the thinking behind it.

A) 105TH CONGRESS

The regulation of non-sports betting has generally been left to the states,[142] each of which has approached the issue in differing ways, from the permissive laws of Nevada[143] and New Jersey,[144] to the prohibitions in Utah[145] and Hawaii.[146] However, when the spectacle of internet gambling[147] began to make headlines in the news in late 1996 right before the start of the 105th Congress, Senator Jon Kyl, a Republican from Arizona, introduced one of the first Internet gambling prohibition bills in March 1997[148]. The bill was simplistic in nature and its main thrust

---

[139.] I. NELSON ROSE AND MARTIN D. OWENS, INTERNET GAMING LAW, (2005) at 192.
[140.] Seth Gorman & Anthony Loo, *Black Jack or Bust: Can U.S. Law Stop Internet Gambling?*, 16 LOY. L.A. ENT. L. J. 667–9 (1996).
[141.] *Id.*
[142.] CHARLES DOYLE, INTERNET GAMBLING 52 (Novinka Books, 2003): "The legality and regulation of gambling is first and foremost a matter of state law that varies considerably from state to state."
[143.] *See* NEV. REV. STATS. 171.015, 194.020, 195.020, 463.0129, 463.01365, 463.01463, 463.01473, 463.0152, 463.0153, 463.016425, 463.160, 463.360, 465.092, NEV. REV. STATS. 465.093, and 465.094.
[144.] *See* N.J. CRIM. LAW 2A 40-1,2,5,6; 2C 37-2; and N.J. CONST.
[145.] *See* UTAH CODE 76-2-202, and 76-10-1101 through 76-10-1108.
[146.] *See* HAW. STATS. § 712–1220 through § 712–1231.
[147.] Note: This section refers to legislation regarding internet gambling in general rather than internet poker specifically. <u>Generally</u> speaking, any of the bills discussed shall not only encompass internet "table" games such as blackjack and roulette, but also internet poker. Within federal law, there is never any great distinction between the two. However, among state law, factors such as "skill" may differentiate the games. Please see the introduction to the section "Existing Law" for a more complete discussion of this topic.
[148.] S. 474: "Internet Gambling Prohibition Act of 1997"

was to prohibit the acceptance of internet wagers.[149] As most internet sites operated offshore, this bill would have had very little impact. Therefore, later redrafts of the bill subjected U.S.-based Internet Service Providers (ISPs)[150] that allowed access to internet gambling websites to "notice and takedown procedures," and also forbade these ISPs from allowing their customers to access websites which U.S. law enforcement determined to contain internet gambling material.[151] Senator Kyl added one of these later redrafts to an appropriations bill, but it was subsequently removed during a House-Senate conference on the bill.

B) 106TH CONGRESS

In 1999, during the 106th Congress, and shortly after the release of the report by the National Gambling Impact Study Commission ("NGISC"), which recommended a ban on internet gambling,[152] Senator Kyl again introduced a bill that focused on ISPs.[153] However, this time there was initial opposition to the bill from various land based gaming interests that wanted exemptions from the bill's application. The horse racing industry had what they thought was an exemption from the Wire Act[154] which had allowed states to compact to allow interstate wagers on horse races from off-track betting facilities, and pursuant to that began to accept internet wagers as well.[155] To accommodate them, Senator Kyl put an exemption in his new bill for horse racing. The bill also contained a similar exemption for pari-mutual gaming (jai alai, dog-racing, etc.). The bill was held up for an extended period of time because Native American tribes wanted their own exemption; in the end, the bill granted a small exemption to the tribes that allowed them to run internet pool wagering and progressive slots. On the last day of the 1999 Congressional session, the Senate passed S.692 by a voice vote.

In 2000, Representative Bob Goodlatte, a Republican from Virginia, introduced the companion bill in the House of Representatives.[156] H.R.3125 received even more scrutiny from land based gambling interests, as state run lotteries lobbied for exemptions as well. However, convenience stores (which wanted to prevent states from selling tickets directly to consumers through the internet) ardently opposed any exemption for state lotteries. Additionally, the Native American gaming interests sought more far-reaching exemption language than they received in the Senate bill. Given the large number of carve-outs the various gaming interests created, the bill seemed to authorize more gambling than it prohibited and thus was defeated in the House.

[149.] Technically, it also prohibits the making of interstate internet wagers as well, see Doyle, *supra* 142 at 44.

[150.] "An Internet service provider (ISP, also called Internet access provider) is a business or organization that offers users access to the Internet and related services." Many but not all ISPs are telephone companies. "They provide services such as Internet transit, domain name registration and hosting, dial-up or DSL access, leased line access and colocation." *See* http://en.wikipedia.org/wiki/Internet_service_provider

[151.] *See* S.AMDT. 3266 to S.2260. For text that closely mirrors the text of Senator Kyl's original bill, see H.R. 2380 introduced by Representative Goodlatte.

[152.] *See* Doyle, *supra* note 142 at 52.

[153.] S. 692.

[154.] The Wire Act prohibits receiving certain bets on sporting events through telephones/internet across state lines where it is illegal at the point of origin. See "Existing Law" Section page 28 infra.

[155.] Senate Hearing II, at 4 (prepared statement of Senator McConnell); House Hearing (testimony of Douglas Donn, Gulfstream Park Racing Association). See also http://www.house.gov/list/press/va06_goodlatte/061106.html

[156.] H.R. 3125.

At the end of the year, Representative Jim Leach, a Republican from Iowa, decided to try a different approach. Leach, the Chairman of the House Banking Committee, proposed a bill[157] which would essentially prohibit credit card companies from processing payment for any illegal internet wager; however it did not define what an "illegal wager" was.[158] The U.S. banking and financial services industries opposed the bill, and the 106th Congress adjourned before any further action could be taken on it.

C) 107TH CONGRESS

During 2001, the beginning of the 107th Congress, neither the House nor the Senate gave the internet gambling issue much attention. Then, after the terrorist attacks of September 11, 2001, the landscape changed dramatically. Members of the House Financial Services Committee[159] became wary that terrorists might use internet gambling accounts as a money laundering device.[160] In response to the attacks, Congress passed the Patriot Act,[161] which dealt with many domestic security needs including the terrorist money laundering issue. The process of creating the Patriot Act was an iterative one and Representative Oxley, a Republican from Ohio, attached the Leach legislation to several iterations of the Patriot Act. However, the House removed the Leach credit card based internet gambling prohibition from the final version of the Patriot Act after vehement lobbying by banking, Native American, and Internet gaming interests.[162]

Shortly after the passage of the Patriot Act absent an internet gambling prohibition, the House Financial Services Committee reported a free-standing version of the Leach bill[163], and sought immediate consideration by the full House.[164] However, this time, the American Gaming Association ("AGA") lobbied for a carve-out to exclude the bill's application to the payment processing of "any lawful transaction with a state-licensed entity."[165] This exemption was granted, and immediately it drew scrutiny from the National Native American Gaming Association (NIGA) which wanted its own carve-out.

Because the Leach legislation provided for civil and criminal penalties, it was referred to the House Judiciary Committee. The Judiciary Committee struck all carve-outs in the bill and reported it to the House floor[166]. However, in late 2002, after the banking industry[167] removed

---

[157] H.R. 4419: "To prevent the use of certain bank instruments for Internet gambling, and for other purposes."

[158] The bill did define what a wager is, just not what an "illegal" wager is. However, it is unclear based on the test of this bill whether a "wager" is made by transferring money to an internet poker site. On an internet poker site, you are simply transferring money from the credit card/bank account to a virtual account on the poker site. Is this a wager? In this instance, money is never directly bet on any event directly from the credit card.

[159] At the start of the 107th Congress the House Banking Committee was renamed the House Financial Services Committee.

[160] See House Committee on Financial Services Report (http://financialservices.house.gov/News.asp?FormMode=release&ID=879) (last visited January 9, 2006) and USA Patriot Act: A review for the Purpose of Reauthorization: House Judiciary Committee, 109th Congress 128–9, April 6, 2005. [hereinafter Patriot].

[161] H.R. 3162.

[162] See Patriot supra note 160 at 137.

[163] H.R.556 (Reps. Leach and LaFace), 148 Cong.Rec. H6848

[164] See H.R. 556.

[165] See id.

[166] H.R. 3125.

its strong objections to the bill, the House Republican leadership put forth the original version of the bill, complete with carve-outs, which passed by a voice vote shortly before the Congressional session ended, such that it was too late for the Senate to act on the bill.

D) 108TH CONGRESS

Given the modicum of success the Leach bill had in 2002, at the start of the 108th Congress, Representative Leach introduced H.R.21[168], which was identical to the bill that passed the House in the previous session. The bill was quickly reported by the House Financial Services Committee, but when it was received by the Judiciary Committee, Representative Chris Cannon, a Republican from Utah, offered an amendment, backed by Native American and e-gaming interests to remove the state carve-outs, which the Committee narrowly adopted.[169]

In response, Representative Spencer Bachus, a Republican from Alabama, introduced H.R.2143[170] which was identical to H.R.21 except for the fact that it omitted the clauses which gave the Judiciary Committee jurisdiction. Eventually, in June 2003, H.R.2143 was passed by the full House of Representatives.[171]

Shortly after the House passage, Senate Banking Committee Chairman Richard Shelby, a Republican from Alabama, held a hearing on the internet gambling issue. For the next month, the Committee held meetings with the various stakeholders in an attempt to reach a consensus on language for the bill, which would be agreeable to all parties, especially the AGA and NIGA.[172] It became clear that the AGA and NIGA's interests were directly opposed, so Senator Shelby reported a bill with no-carve outs (S.627).[173] Once the bill reported, the Nevada Senators, being aligned with the AGA, placed "holds" on the bill, thereby expressing their opposition.

In mid-2004, after a WTO ruling that the U.S.'s anti-internet gaming stance violated international law,[174] the United States Chamber of Commerce (USCC), the largest business lobby in the U.S., sent a letter to the Senate voicing its opposition to the internet gambling prohibition bill. Due to the stringent opposition of the AGA, NIGA, and USCC, the Senate never took a vote on the bill.[175]

---

[167] House Report 107–339—Part 1—Unlawful Internet Gambling Funding Prohibition Act, 107th Congress, Judiciary Committee, 1st Session.
[168] H.R. 21.
[169] *See generally, id.* ; House Report 108–051—Part 2—Unlawful Internet Gambling Funding Prohibition Act, 108th Congress, Judiciary Committee, 2nd Session.
[170] H.R. 2143.
[171] *Id.*
[172] *See generally* Senate Report 108–173—Internet Gambling Funding Prohibition Act.
[173] S. 627
[174] Please see the following section "Existing Law" for a more complete description of the WTO's ruling.
[175] Many, many thanks to Mr. Dan Walsh of Greenberg, Traurig LLP for providing me with the background for this legislation section, as well as much of the language for this section, which I used, with permission.

E) 109TH CONGRESS

Many commentators initially believed that the chance for a ban of internet gambling died after the Senate failed to pass S.627.[176] However, due to the recent Jack Abramoff scandal, the campaign against internet gambling not only has new life but seems to be thriving. Jack Abramoff, a formerly powerful Washington lobbyist, pled guilty to fraud and conspiracy counts in early 2006 in connection with, among other things, a $50,000 bribe he gave to "the wife of an unnamed congressional staffer in return for the staffer's help in killing an Internet gambling measure."[177]

Mr. Abramoff worked at the firms of Preston Gates & Ellis LLP and subsequently Greenberg, Traurig, LLP. His primary client was eLottery, Inc. that generated its profits by helping states and other organizations put their lotteries online. After Senator Kyl's Bill, S.692 passed the Senate in late 1999, eLottery was in a panic. eLottery hired Mr. Abramoff to defeat the companion bill introduced by Representative Goodlatte, H.R.3125.[178]

The Goodlatte bill appeared to be "on its way to passage by an overwhelming margin in the House of Representatives."[179] However, Tony Rudy, a senior aide to then-Majority Whip Tom DeLay, a Republican from Texas, helped dash the bill in the House. According to the Washington Post, Mr. Rudy e-mailed Abramoff internal congressional communications. In return, Mr. Abramoff gave him expensive trips and other luxury items. Abramoff successfully used Rudy to convince anti-gambling conservative representatives that the carve-outs defeated the central purpose of the bill. Additionally, "Abramoff quietly arranged for eLottery to pay conservative, anti-gambling activists to help in the firm's $2 million pro-gambling campaign, including Ralph Reed, former head of the Christian Coalition, and the Rev. Louis P. Sheldon of the Traditional Values Coalition."[180] He even went so far as to circulate a fake letter by Florida Governor Jeb Bush that purportedly said that Governor Bush opposed the bill because it infringed on states' rights.[181]

Even though Representative Goodlatte "had more than enough votes" for his bill to pass, he was worried that all the commotion surrounding the bill would cause unwanted amendments to be proposed. Therefore, in order to avoid a floor fight on the bill, he placed it on the suspension calendar, which banned amendments, but at the same time required a two-thirds vote for the bill to pass. Abramoff exploited this opportunity and managed to scurry up enough votes to defeat the bill.[182]

In the recent wake of the discovery of Abramoff's illegal activities, Representative Goodlatte and others appear to feel cheated out of a legislative victory. Those Republicans who previously voted against the bill likely feel duped and are possibly more inclined to vote for a

---

[176.] See, e.g., Allyn Jaffrey Shulman, 2003 Legal Overview 1995-Present, CARDPLAYER MAGAZINE ONLINE, October 1, 2003, http://www.cardplayer.com/poker_magazine/archives/?a_id=13571.

[177.] Susan Schmidt and James V. Grimaldi, *Abramoff Pleads Guilty to 3 Counts: Lobbyist to Testify About Lawmakers in Corruption Probe*, WASHINGTON POST, January 4, 2006 at A01. (http://www.washingtonpost.com/wp-dyn/content/article/2006/01/03/AR2006010300474.html)

[178.] Susan Schmidt and James V. Grimaldi, *How a Lobbyist Stacked the Deck: Abramoff Used DeLay Aide, Attacks on Allies to Defeat Anti-Gambling Bill*, WASHINGTON POST, October 16, 2005 at Page A01. (http://www.washingtonpost.com/wp-dyn/content/article/2005/10/15/AR2005101501539.html).

[179.] *Id.*
[180.] *Id.*
[181.] *Id.*
[182.] *Id.*

new version of it. Furthermore, given that illegal means were used to defeat the original bill, those who proposed it feel even more morally justified in their anti-internet gambling stance. Therefore, the political climate was ripe for the passage of an internet gambling prohibition.

Two bills were introduced in the House at the start of the next Congressional session. Representative Goodlatte introduced H.R.4777 in February 2006.[183] Representative Leach introduced H.R.4411 during the first 109th Congressional session.[184] Goodlatte's bill is a throwback to the Kyl legislation and focuses on ISPs. It is generally cleaner legislation and includes a prohibition on hyperlinking.[185] It also allocates $10 million per year for the investigation of internet gambling by the DOJ. Leach's bill is similar to his previous legislation in that it targets the payment processing mechanism for illegal internet wagers. This version contains carve-outs for horse racing and fantasy sports. The Leach Bill, H.R. 4411 passed the House of Representatives by a vote of 317–93 in July, 2006.[186] Given the legislative climate, many commentators believed that H.R. 4411 would have been passed by the Senate and the U.S. would finally have taken direct action against internet gambling.[187] However, 4411 was sent back to committees and not put up for a vote in the final week that the 109th Congress was in session. For all intents and purposes, this bill was dead.

Then, out of the blue, three days before Congress's session was set to close, Republican leadership in Congress debated adding "last-minute provisions to a major maritime security bill, including the court security and online gambling legislation that Republican leaders sought unsuccessfully" to add the 2007 fiscal year defense authorization bill.[188] Republican leadership did in fact add an "unlawful internet gambling enforcement" provision to the Safe Port Act.[189] They did so without sending the bill back to committee, thus "preventing Democrats adding amendments to the final conference agreement on the bill," prompting outrage among Democrats.[190] Congress passed the Safe Port Security Act, and President Bush signed into law on October 13, 2006.[191]

The Port Security Bill was the last bill to pass the 109th Congress. While this bill passed by a vote of 98-0, several Democrats were enraged. Some Democrats claim that the Senators were not even allowed to see the final language of the bill before it was put to a vote.[192] They

---

[183] H.R. 4777.

[184] H.R. 4411.

[185] Hyperlinking means having a link on a website which a user can click on to get to another website, in this case one that contains gambling. This is especially important in the internet poker industry because, as mentioned above, poker sites run both real money sites and play money sites. The play money sites often have different internet addresses and the play money webpages contain hyperlinking to the real money pages. For more on this see the "Advertising" section.

[186] *House Approves Goodlatte Legislation to Combat Illegal Gambling*, http://www.house.gov/list/press/va06_goodlatte/061106.html

[187] *Id.*

[188] *Internet Gambling Bill may be added to Port Security Bill*, EYE ON GAMBLING, (http://www.eog.com/news/industry.aspx?id=9184) (hereinafter EYE)

[189] H.R. 4954

[190] EYE, *supra* note 188.

[191] H.R. 4954 and *Congress Approves Internet Gambling Bill* (http://today.reuters.com/news/articlenews.aspx?type=internetNews&storyID=2006-09-30T045429Z_01_N29415181_RTRUKOC_0_US-CONGRESS-TECH-GAMBLING.xml&WTmodLoc=InternetNewsHome_C1_%5BFeed%5D-2)

[192] *See* I. Nelson Rose, *The New Law Broken Down* (http://www.pocketfives.com/68CBB9B1-C383-45BF-8308-13BBFE1C37BC.aspx) (hereinafter New Law)

accused the Republicans of clandestinely attaching the internet gambling bill to a national security bill that absolutely had to pass.[193]

VI) THE SAFE PORT ACT OF 2006

The "unlawful internet gambling enforcement" provision of the Safe Port Act is the weakest form of anti-internet gambling legislation proposed to date. In summary, this entire bill does make it illegal to own or operate an internet gambling site; something that the US government has claimed has been illegal since its inception. More specifically, §5363 of this act states that "No person engaged in the business of betting or wagering may knowingly accept" any form of payment, credit cards, money orders, checks, for the purpose of pursuing illegal gambling. Section 5364 of the act gives the Fed 270 days to establish a system of regulations to identify illegal gambling websites and promulgate rules to prevent them from receiving funds. "The regulations will require everyone connected with a 'designated payment system' to identify and block all restricted transactions."[194]

While the bill makes operating an internet poker site illegal, unlike previous iterations of anti-online gambling legislation, it does not contain a specific enforcement mechanism such as making it illegal for credit card companies to transfer funds to restricted sites[195] or making it illegal for ISPs to allow the American populace access to these sites. Rather, it instructs the Federal Reserve (the 'Fed') to make rules needed to enforce the law. Presumably, the Fed will populate a list of restricted gambling websites and pass regulations forbidding US credit card companies and banks from processing payments to these sites.

The most important question to ask regarding this new law is how does the jurisdictional analysis discussed above applies. The answer is the same. Our government does not have the authority to enforce this law outside the boundaries of the United States. This law allows the government to prevent credit card companies and other financial institutions from sending money from customers' accounts to PartyPoker, PokerStars, and other online gaming companies. However, the question remains, is this enough to shut down internet poker in the United States?

The short answer is no. Two large loopholes remain which allow Americans continued access to online gaming. First, one could set up a bank account offshore, such as in Canada, and then transfer funds from this account to the poker website of his choice. Second, and perhaps more importantly, this law is not crafted narrowly enough to stop "business as usual" in the online poker world. This bill only gives the government the power to make rules preventing U.S. financial institutions from transferring money to persons or business engaged in the business of betting or wagering online, i.e. internet gambling sites. It does not give the U.S. government the power to prevent the money from being sent from U.S. citizens to non-gambling related institutions. As explained above, one of the most common ways a player gets money from his account to a poker site is to first transfer it to a middleman such as Neteller and then transfer it

---

[193] All the Democrats' objections can best be captured by listening to Rep. Shelly Bakus speech on the house floor at http://www.youtube.com/watch?v=nb1pzayqPaI

[194] *See* New Law, *supra* note 192.

[195] *See* Earl Burton, *Noted Legal Expert I. Nelson Rose's Views On Recent Legislation*: "Payment processors are not covered, unless prosecutors want to use theories of aiding and abetting. Treasury will make new regulations to require money transferors to identify and block funds from gambling sites. Banks will thus not be required to read paper checks."
(http://www.pokernews.com/news/2006/10/nelson-rose-views-legislation.htm)

from Neteller to the overseas site. Neteller is a legitimate financial company and does not engage in the business of gambling. Therefore, the Safe Port Act does not and cannot prohibit a credit card company or bank from allowing a U.S. citizen to transfer his funds to Neteller. Moreover, since Neteller is not a U.S. company, this act then does not prohibit Neteller from transferring these funds to an online gambling site. Furthermore, since this law does not apply to players, players are not prohibited from sending money to Neteller or to the internet sites themselves.[196] Thus, legally, given the manner in which this law is written and its jurisdictional reach, the Safe Port Act should have little impact on internet gambling.

However, what is true legally is not always what happens in reality. Several internet poker vendors, particularly those that are publicly traded, have decided to close their doors to American consumers. PartyGaming, in an effort to "comply with the spirit of American law," was one of the first companies to announce that it no longer would process wagers from American citizens.[197] Upon announcing this decision, Party Gaming's value dropped from $12 billion to $7 billion, and its stock plummeted an amazing 58 percent.[198] The future of Party Gaming is in jeopardy as well, largely due to the fact that prior to its decision to pull out of the U.S. market, 80 percent of its revenue was generated from the United States.[199] Other sites have followed Party Poker's lead and bowed out of the U.S. market including Paradise Poker, Pacific Poker, and the financial intermediary Firepay.[200] Other industry giants, however, such as FullTilt Poker and PokerStars have chosen to continue business as usual.[201] Given that these companies are located offshore and can legally receive funds from U.S. players transferred through Neteller and similar intermediaries, it is not likely that the internet poker landscape will change extensively in the near future. Thus, the Safe Port Act, aside from scaring some players out of the market, has had, and will likely have, little effect on internet gambling.

Now that this paper has established the current status of the legality of online poker, namely that it isn't legal for operators but that there is little or nothing the government can do about it do to jurisdictional issues, it will analyze the reasons behind the US government's opposition to online gambling, consider the pros and cons of legalizing and regulating online poker, and finally make recommendations as to how the government should proceed with respect to the online poker industry in the future.

VII) THE PUBLIC POLICY REASONS BEHIND THE U.S. GOVERNMENT'S DISLIKE OF ONLINE GAMING

On Wednesday, December 15, 2005 a man walked into a Wachovia bank branch in Lehigh, Pennsylvania and handed the bank teller a note claiming he was carrying and gun and demanding all the money in the teller's drawer. A few minutes later he walked out with almost $3000 of the bank's money and a few days later the police arrested and charged him with bank

---

[196] *See, e.g.,* Allyn Shulman, What's NOT included in Anti-Gambling Legislation: A Legal Perspective (http://www.cardplayer.com/poker_news/article/1446) (last visited February 18, 2006)

[197] *See* Jonathan Laing, *Last Woman Standing,* BARRON'S ONLINE (http://online.barrons.com/public/article/SB116018480631785723-E7nqJqKei44PIzfxJ_qCG7gnerk_20061106.html?mod=mktw) (hereinafter Woman) and *Online Poker Industry responds to Law Change* (http://www.cardplayer.com/poker_news/article/3261).

[198] *See* Woman, *supra* note 202.

[199] *Id.*

[200] *See* http://www.neverwinpoker.com/phpnuke/html/ftopict-27922.html

[201] *Id.*

robbery. The identity of this master criminal shocked the community. Police identified Greg Hogan, 19 year-old son of a Baptist minister and president of the 2008 undergraduate class of Lehigh University, as the perpetrator. Mr. Hogan claimed his gambling addiction drove him to rob the bank[202] after he lost over $5,000 in the previous few months playing online poker.[203]

This is just one example that internet poker opponents use as an illustration of the negative effects that the game, and internet gambling in general, have on our society. For the last several hundred years, "Americans have vacillated between their desires to permit and control gambling, creating an erratic record of legalized gaming initiatives and a distasteful legacy of illegal gaming and corruption."[204] For example, gambling is fully legal in Nevada, unlawful in Tennessee, and legal only if licensed and on water in Illinois.[205] Sometimes our government's and our society's opinion on the ill effects of gambling seems to have no rhyme or reason. While society's opinion of the pros and cons of internet poker are substantially similar to its opinion of gambling in the real world, online gaming does raise a few new objections.[206]

Some of the most common critiques of online gaming, which are not used against land based gaming, include: 1) increased operating hours—internet gaming can occur 24 hours a day, 7 days a week; 2) frequency and speed of gaming—many more hands per hour in the case of poker and bets per hour in the case of table games and slots occur online as compared to in brick and mortar casinos;[207] 3) variety of games—by allowing free trials of games, the internet facilitates learning new games and thus more gambling; 4) amount of money players—in general, the bet size can be less on the internet, thus attracting people with lower income;[208] and 5) greater social accessibility—because no social interaction is necessary on the internet, socially awkward people are more likely to begin gambling.[209] Aside from these concerns, online gambling critics cite deeper problems.

One of the most prevalent complaints anti-gambling authorities have is that the availability of gambling leads to addiction in many people which in turn leads to negative externalities on society.[210] In fact, the only reason cited in the Safe Port Act for banning online

---

[202] *Gambling Blamed in Bank Rob Case*, CBS NEWS ONLINE. Hogan's lawyer says "His gambling addiction led him to make a terrible, terrible mistake." (http://www.cbsnews.com/stories/2005/12/14/national/main1127469.shtml)

[203] *See generally*, *Gambling Blamed in Bank Rob Case*, CBS NEWS ONLINE, http://www.cbsnews.com/stories/2005/12/14/national/main1127469.shtml; Alan Roarty, *Class of 2008 President Arrested in Bank Robbery*, THE BROWN AND WHITE, LEHIGH UNIVERSITY STUDENT NEWSPAPER, Dec. 15, 2005 http://bw.lehigh.edu/story.asp?ID=19305; and
http://www.neverwinpoker.com/phpnuke/html/modules.php?name=Forums&file=viewtopic&t=11181.

[204] *See* DAVID G. SCHWARTZ, CUTTING THE WIRE: GAMBLING PROHIBITION AND THE INTERNET (Univ. Nevada Press, 2005) at 12.

[205] *Id.* at 12.

[206] *See* Mark G. Tratos, *Gaming on the Internet III: The Politics of Internet Gaming and the Genesis of Legal Bans or Licensing*, 610 PLI/PAT 711, June 2000 at 752-3: "At the heart of the opposition to Internet gaming is the general opposition to gambling per se. Until the second half of the 20th Century, gambling in America was considered immoral by much of the population. Whether this moral stigma was the result of religious condemnation or *753 prevailing social attitudes is unclear."

[207] In online poker players can "multi-table"- which means they can play at several, occasional upwards of 6, tables at the same time.

[208] At a casino, the smallest stakes one normally can find is $1-$2. Online, poker sites often offer games as small at $.05 -$.1

[209] *Id.*

[210] *See* National Gambling Impact Study Commission, Final Report, at 1-1 and 5-4,5 http://govinfo.library.unt.edu/ngisc/reports/fullrpt.html [hereinafter NGIS].

gaming is that it leads to "debt collection problems" for U.S. financial institutions.[211] The sad story of Greg Hogan is an example of another type of externality. Internet gambling opponents say that along with the increased access to gambling which the internet now provides will come a dramatic increase in the number of problem gamblers our society must support and deal with. Problem gambling results in negative spillovers onto the rest of society. An increase in crime is a notable example.[212] Lost work and school hours, which result in lower societal efficiency, are another. An increase in personal debt and therefore the need for state public assistance is a third.[213]

Another common complaint that anti-gambling advocates lodge against casinos is that they allow access to minors too easily.[214] This complaint translates to online gambling as well. In a casino, a minor may enter with fake identification. Online, it is even easier for underage gamblers to play. First, the "legal" or rather, "allowed," gambling age by most internet card rooms is 18, while it is 21 in most brick-and-mortar casinos.[215] Second, online casinos do very little to verify the age of the players on their websites. Most casinos simply ask the player to input his or her birthday when signing up for an account. Then all a player needs to do is transfer money onto the site using a credit card or wire transfer. Underage gamblers who lie about their age and have access to their own funds, or their parent's credit cards, can easily play online poker without anyone being the wiser.[216] State governments make a similar complaint, namely that online gambling restricts the State's ability to set social policy. When online casinos offer a certain type of game or permit people of a certain age to gamble, they thereby cut off the State's ability to set that policy.

Aside from the social evils associated with all gambling, critics of online gambling believe that internet gaming has even more negative elements than traditional gambling. First, the government cites the argument that because online gaming is done offshore, it cannot ensure that these sites are run fairly. The government cannot intercede to audit these gaming sites, there is no government protection against these sites using their software to cheat players, and there is no gaming board to resolve customer disputes.[217] For example, the designer of a blackjack software program could have his card generator give the dealer blackjack every time a player doubles down[218], thus reaping a huge profit for the casino. If a player has a dispute against any of these offshore internet casinos, the best he can do is bring suit in the nation the site is incorporated in. If this is in England, he may have a fair shot, but if it is in a country with

---

[211] Safe Port Act H.R. 4954
[212] NGIS, *supra* note 215 at 5-5.
[213] *See* I. Nelson Rose, *The Law of Internet Gambling*, GAMBLING AND THE LAW, http://www.gamblingandthelaw.com/internet.html.
[214] *See* NGIS, *supra* note 210, at 5-4.
[215] *See generally* http://www.gambling-law-us.com/State-Laws/ for state laws, and www.pokerstars, or other sites for online ages (The way pokerstars.com and partypoker.com work in terms of age restrictions is that once you download their software you are required to register for an account- name, location, etc. They also ask for your birth date. All you need do is enter a birth date that shows that you are at least 18 years of age. This age limit corresponds with the age limit in the country where the site is located- England, Costa Rica, etc).
[216] *See Underage Internet Gambling Study: Children as Young as 11 Can Set Up Gambling Accounts at the Click of a Button*, July 27, 2004, http://www.gamcare.org.uk/shownews.php/000095.html.
[217] *See, generally,* NGIS, *supra* note 210.
[218] "Double down: Double the wager, take exactly one more card, and then stand." *See* http://en.wikipedia.org/wiki/Blackjack.

an antiquated legal system, hope is all but lost.[219] Even if the player did manage to get the corporation into court, given that there is no oversight of the online casino to begin with, it would be very hard to gather enough proof against the company to win the case.

There have been two recent examples of how a lack of governmental or other oversight has caused poker players to lose substantial sums of money. PokerSpot.com, one of the first online cardrooms, designed by poker pro Dutch Boyd, went defunct shortly after it opened.[220] There are two stories circulating surrounding the demise of this corporation. The story put forth by Mr. Boyd is that the credit card processing service it used to process customer deposits, Net Pro,[221] either didn't process the transactions quickly enough for the company to have adequate funds or it kept some of the money for itself when it should not have.[222] The other story is that because PokerSpot did not have adequate working capital, the company used the players' deposits, meant for their personal poker gambling, to run the day to day operations of the business.[223] Either way, it is agreed that at some point in time shortly after the launch of the PokerSpot.com, it went defunct and did not have enough cash to refund to the players all of their deposits.[224] Given the lack of regulation in the industry, and the fact that the U.S. government had no jurisdiction or standing to intervene, the players were left high and dry.[225]

The second example involves a twenty-one year old professional internet poker player named Justin Bonomo who goes by the internet poker screen name "zeejustin".[226] PokerStars and PartyPoker accused Justin, along with several other high profile internet poker players, of "multi-tabling" big buy-in tournament events. "Multi-tabling," in this instance, means that Justin entered an online poker tournament using two (or more) different poker screen names.[227] That is the real world equivalent of entering the same poker tournament as two different people, which, of course, is physically impossible. "Multi-tabling" is cheating according to online poker room rules. PokerStars searched it records and itemized the money Justin won as a result of multi-tabling ($3,445.75) and redistributed it to other players in the tournament. PartyPoker, on the other hand, froze Justin's entire account and kept over $100,000, which they could not prove was earned as a result of multi-tabling, for themselves (no redistribution).[228] Again, Justin has little or no recourse because the site is not governed by U.S. policy.

[219.] *See* I. Nelson Rose, *The Law of Internet Gambling*, GAMBLING AND THE LAW, http://www.gamblingandthelaw.com/internet.html. Professor Rose notes "Government oversight of these gaming operations are also often spotty or non-existent. Players have little guarantee that the games are run honestly, they will be paid if they win, or even that they can get their front money returned."

[220.] www.pokerspot.com.

[221.] The equivalent of Neteller or Firepay.

[222.] *See* http://www.dutchboyd.com/blog/2004/12/pokerspot.html and http://www.rakefree.com/faq10.htm#faq [hereinafter Boyd].

[223.] *See* http://extempore.livejournal.com/76520.html and http://archiveserver.twoplustwo.com/showthreaded.php?Cat=0&Board=&Number=567339&page=2&view=&sb=5&o=0&fpart (last visited April 19, 2006)

[224.] *See* Boyd, *supra* note 222.

[225.] Antigua, where pokerspot.com was allegedly incorporated, disclaims licensing the organization. *See* http://www.antiguagaming.gov.ag/press/Press_Release_pkspot.asp.

[226.] www.zeejustin.com

[227] *See* footnote 212 for other definition.

[228.] *See* http://www.zeejustin.com/journal.php?journal_id=81; http://www.neverwinpoker.com/phpnuke/html/modules.php?name=Forums&file=viewtopic&t=17789; and http://www.neverwinpoker.com/phpnuke/html/modules.php?name=News&file=article&sid=438&mode

Another reason that States dislike online gaming is that online gambling takes away from their annual revenues. States that allow land based gambling usually collect a fairly high tax on wagers placed at these casinos through either a privately negotiated contract with the casino or through a statute that mandates a wager tax.[229] States also collect revenue from gambling programs they run themselves such as a statewide lottery drawing or scratch off lottery tickets. Before online gambling, the state run lotteries might have been the only game in town.

Another reason the government dislikes online gambling more than land based gambling is because of tax reporting requirements, or in this case, the lack of tax reporting requirements. For a land based casino, IRS regulations require that for poker tournament cashes, the casino file a report with the IRS and withhold taxes from a player if he wins greater than $600 or more than 300 times his initial wager.[230] There are other reporting requirements as well.[231] Online casinos are not subject to any such reporting requirements. They are not required to provide the U.S. government with information about the monies U.S. citizens win or lose on their poker sites. Thus, assuming players do not completely follow the honor system, the government loses the tax revenue that players earn online and fail to report.

Last, States claim that online poker interferes with their autonomy.[232] As it stands now, each state is allowed to determine whether to allow gambling within its borders, and if so, what types of gambling to allow. As stated above, states such as Utah and Tennessee completely outlaw gambling, while it is nearly 100 percent permissible in Nevada. States such as Connecticut allow it, but only on tribal land. Each state is different. Internet gambling threatens this. By breaking down the boundaries between space and elevating each player into the realm of cyberspace, a player from New York can "sit" with a player from Guam and a player from Utah at the same virtual poker table. Internet gambling has essentially "nationalized" the gambling industry, removing almost all individual state nuances. For all intents and purposes, unless States are going to crackdown and begin arresting their own citizens for placing bets on the internet, States no longer have any say about what is legal is terms of gambling within their borders. If internet gambling is going to be stopped, the government needs to target either ISPs or credit card companies. Further, targeting these middlemen almost has to be done on a national level. Congress will have to wield the mighty axe of the Commerce Clause to pass legislation prohibiting, or regulating internet gambling. Thus, internet gambling will have to have a standardized national policy, stripping the states of their autonomy in deciding which facets to allow and which to proscribe.[233]

=&order=0&thold=0 for description of how JJProdigy, another online poker pro, whom online poker sites also caught multi-tabling.

[229] *See, generally,* David H. Lantzer, *Internet Gaming Tax Regulation: Can Old Laws Learn New Tricks?*, CHAPMAN LAW REVIEW, Spring 2002. For example of statute, *see* Federal Wager Tax; I.R.C. § 4401. The Federal Excise Wagering Tax allows the federal government to collect a tax equal to 0.25 percent of the amount of any state authorized wager.

[230] *See, e.g.,* Russ Fox, *Tax Aspects of Online Gambling,* (http://www.gambling-law-us.com/Articles-Notes/online-gambling-tax.htm,.

[231] *Id.*

[232] *See, e.g.,* Earl Burton, *Washington State Passes Online Poker and Gaming Legislation*, POKER NEWS, May 2, 2006, http://www.pokernews.com/news/2006/5/washington-state-online-poker-legislation.htm: discussing how states are taking measures against online gaming because it interferes with already existing prohibitions on gambling.

[233] *See* NGIS, *supra* note 210, at 5-9: "several states have concluded that only the federal government has the potential to regulate or prohibit Internet gambling."

While internet poker has its detractors, it also has a huge number of proponents. These proponents admonish the states for speaking out against internet gambling while at the same time permitting land based gambling and lotteries within the state.[234] These players enjoy playing poker in the comfort of their own homes without having to drive out of state to find a casino. Furthermore, it is often more economical to play online because the casinos charge a smaller rake, spread smaller stakes games, and offer rakeback.[235] Moreover, many players actually contend that online poker reduces crime, specifically organized crime and bookmaking.[236] In states where casinos do not exist, many players play at underground card clubs, which are illegal to own and operate. For example, ARod was caught in a New York City cardclub that allegedly had mafia ties.[237] Online sites present players with a safer way to play poker and thus cut down on organized crime's business. The last, and most substantial, argument made in support of online gaming is simply that reasonable people should be allowed to make up their own minds about whether they wish to gamble. Players feel that Big Brother should stop looking over their shoulder and telling them that gambling is morally, fiscally, or otherwise wrong.[238] They want to be allowed to make up their own minds.

VIII) THE PROS AND CONS OF LEGALIZING AND REGULATING ONLINE POKER

The 104th United States Congress charged the National Gambling Impact Study Commission with, among other things, investigating the causes of a large growth in gambling in the past several decades.[239] Congress specifically asked the Commission to assess the impact of internet gambling on the United States and to recommend steps that Congress should take to combat it.[240] The Commission found that the three biggest reasons that Congress should consider prohibiting internet gambling are because internet gambling is abused by underage gamblers, facilitates addiction for pathological gamblers due to it's high speed and instant gratification, and raises the potential for criminal activities (such as stealing credit card numbers or money laundering).[241] Without discussing at any significant length other

---

[234] *See, e.g.*, THE POKER PLAYERS ALLIANCE, http://www.pokerplayersalliance.org/ [hereinafter PPA].

[235] *See* http://en.wikipedia.org/wiki/Rakeback#R. A program through which a player gets back a certain percentage of the rake he paid to the house. "Rebate/repayment to a player of a portion the rake paid by the player, normally from a non-cardroom, third-party source such as an affiliate."

[236] *See* Clive Small, *Gambling and the Harms We Choose to Have*, NATIONAL GAMBLING REGULATION CONFERENCE, May 1999, http://www.aic.gov.au/conferences/gambling99/small.pdf." Arguably internet gambling reduces organized crime."

[237] *See* AROD, *supra* note 1.

[238] *See* PPA, *supra* note 234.

[239] *See* NGIS, *supra* note 210.

[240] *Id.* at 5-1: "A key mandate of the National Gambling Impact Study Commission was to assess the impact of technology on gambling in the United States."

[241] *Id.* at 5-5.

alternatives, [242] the Commission recommended that Congress take immediate action to prohibit internet gambling[243]

Several commentators suggest that it is a better idea for the U.S. to legalize and regulate internet gambling rather than to forbid it completely.[244] Some even suggest that the ills enumerated by gambling opponents can be better alleviated through regulation than outright prohibition.[245] In April 2000, the Gaming Board for Great Britain recommended that the British government legalize internet poker under a system of permits and regulations and subject the companies to a tax on their gross profits (15 percent was recommended).[246] Great Britain's legalization of internet gaming has caused several leading internet poker sites to go public on the British stock exchange, the most recent of which PokerStars, which is estimated to receive $2

---

[242] *Id.* at 5-12,13: "The Commission recommends to the President, Congress, and the Department of Justice (DOJ) that the federal government should prohibit, without allowing new exemptions or the expansion of existing federal exemptions to other jurisdictions, Internet gambling not already authorized within the United States or among parties in the United States and any foreign jurisdiction. Further, the Commission recommends that the President and Congress direct DOJ to develop enforcement strategies . . ."

[243] In its final report, in the internet gaming section, the commission has a 3-page part entitled "Regulation or Prohibition?" However, little, if any regulation is discussed in the part. The part is essentially devoted to a brief commentary on steps already taken to prohibit, rather than regulate internet gambling. This prohibit includes prosecutions undertaken by the NY AG as well as state legislation designed to eliminate internet gaming.

[244] *See*, Lantzer, *supra* note 234 at 3: "The lure of increased revenue and consumer preference will likely result in federal and state governments enacting legislation to legalize and regulate Internet gaming." "A relatively clean slate encourages governments and businesses to negotiate regulatory solutions that will benefit all parties;" See also http://www.neverwinpoker.com/phpnuke/html/article-451-thread-1-0.html Referring to http://business.timesonline.co.uk/article/0,,9070-2136074,00.html Bryan Micon posting, in response to newspaper reports the PokerStars.com is going to make an IPO on the British stock market for an estimated $2 billion: "Lesson to the USA—look at all these billion dollar companies setting up shop overseas with our money! Fucking regulate online poker and bring these very wealthy companies (with their K's of jobs & M's of taxable revenue) to our country!" [hereinafter Micon]; and Seth Gorman & Antony Loo, *Black Jack or Bust: Can U.S. Law Stop Internet Gambling?*, 16 LOY. L.A. ENT. L. J. 667–9 (1996).: "Moreover, conditional legalization of gambling is consistent with most states' policies that favor gambling. Most states permit gambling in some form or another."

[245] *See* Micon, *id.*

[246] *See* Professor I. Nelson Rose, *Understanding the Law of Internet Gambling*, http://www.gamblingandthelaw.com/internet_gambling.html "The Review Body has already had submitted to it a separate paper prepared by the Gaming Board on this issue [Internet Gambling], following a study carried out by the Board during late 1999/early 2000. The key conclusions of that paper are as follows. There are a growing number of sites on the Internet which offer opportunities to gamble and in particular on-line casino gaming, and legislation in this country bears on Internet gambling in unintended and erratic ways. For instance, no on-line casino gaming site can lawfully be established here, but residents are free to play on overseas sites and those sites can accept bets from here without breaking any British laws. The Board concludes that legislative change is needed to remedy this unsatisfactory situation. It does not believe that measures which attempt to prohibit on-line gambling in Britain would be either sensible or likely to be successful. Thus, whilst acknowledging that legislative change is unlikely to be simple or straightforward, the Board recommends that a coherent legislative system should be established which permits controlled and regulated Internet gambling sites in Britain. It believes that this is a matter to which the Review Body should give particular attention . . ."

billion for its IPO.[247] Additionally, North Dakota proposed a bill to legalize a "licensed internet live poker establishment" and then tax the internet corporations according to a graduated tax schedule; the bill narrowly missed becoming law.[248]

Regulation is capable of both assuaging the social problems surrounding internet gambling mentioned in the previous section and bringing economic and other benefits to the U.S. First, through proper regulation, the U.S. government can prevent the use of internet gambling facilities by unwanted players, namely underage persons and problem gamblers. There are several regulatory models through which the government can do this. The U.S. can mandate that all monetary transfers to internet poker sites come from U.S. bank accounts or U.S. based credit cards. These institutions will be able to properly verify the age of the player well before he deposits money on a poker site—namely when he signs up for a bank account or credit card—by examining his social security number and other government issued identification. Additionally, the U.S. could also set up a protocol, much like the currency transaction reports banks must issue for transactions over $10,000, such that banks or other financial institutions must monitor deposits onto these sites and report habitual or problem gamblers to the proper authorities. The government could also regulate what type of gaming is offered, i.e. slots and poker only, or table games and sports betting only. Moreover, it could empower families to monitor minors or problem gambler encouraging the installation of monitoring chips in computers.[249] Currently, the only safeguards against problem gamblers and minors accessing sites are the ones instituted by the sites themselves, which are, as previously discussed, minimal at best. This type of regulation will work better than the Safe Port Act's prohibition given its jurisdictional problems.[250]

Second, regulation will allow the U.S. government to monitor the integrity of the sites to prevent cheating. It will also allow players and others associated with the internet sites a reputable forum to adjudicate grievances, namely a U.S. federal court. Additionally, the government can mandate each site be audited by an independent authority (PriceWaterHouse, etc.) annually. Private citizens would, of course, have the right to bring civil actions against internet gambling operators in a U.S. court of appropriate U.S. jurisdiction. The U.S. legislature

---

[247] *See* Matthew Goodman, *Pokerstars Reveals Hand with Plans for $1 Billion Pound Float*, THE LONDON TIMES ONLINE, April 16, 2006, http://business.timesonline.co.uk/article/0,,8209-2136074,00.html.

[248] *See* NDHB150 for the 59th Legislative Assembly of North Dakota.

[249] *See* Gorman & Loo, *supra* note 78: "An anti-gambling chip, the "G-chip," for computers, would allow parents to block out Internet services that offer gambling, and thus, prevent minors from gaining access to the virtual casinos. A blocking mechanism would also allow the Internet to develop without governmental interference. The issues of jurisdiction and law enforcement are not raised by this solution because it does not require the application of any law. This solution allows parents to dictate what activities are appropriate for their children to access."

[250] *See* NGIS, *supra* note 210, at 5-10,11: "To effectively prohibit Internet gambling, the U.S. government would have to ensure that these licensed operators do not offer their services within U.S. borders, a proposition that poses a range of unanswered questions regarding feasibility. Efforts to prevent customers in the United States from accessing and using these sites may be easily circumvented. For example, the on-line registration process makes possible an initial screening of customers when they disclose the locations of bank accounts or credit card companies. Yet potential customers can take a number of steps to conceal their location within the United States. For example, patrons can establish offshore bank accounts and wire the money from those accounts to the Internet gambling site. In addition, patrons can mask their origins by first dialing an offshore ISP before logging onto a particular site, thereby creating the appearance of operating in a legal Internet gambling jurisdiction."

can establish whatever penalties it sees fit, from monetary fines to shutdown of the violating website, for violations of these monitoring provisions.

Third, as the NGISC's report fails to mention, the U.S. would receive a massive windfall from tax revenue if it chooses to legalize and tax internet gambling.[251] At a flat tax rate of 6.25%, internet gambling could generate an upwards of $750 million dollars annually. Several other countries have recognized the tax benefits of legalizing and regulating online gaming---Australia, Costa Rica, Great Britain, Aruba, and Antigua just to name a few.[252] Legalized gambling has already proven its effectiveness in raising revenue; for example, in Nevada legalized gambling has led to "one of the longest economic booms any state has experienced," and Las Vegas is currently the country's fastest growing city.[253] In addition to generating millions in revenue for the state, gambling also boosts the economy by creating thousands of jobs. In discussing brick-and-mortar casinos creating economic growth, the Practicing Law Institute comments that "once opened, the new casinos provide tens of thousands of jobs in the service industries, leading to sustained community economic growth. The economics of the gaming industry are such that as in many cash-based businesses, even a largely uneducated work force can enjoy economic prosperity. Thus, the brick and mortar casinos provide a sustaining economic benefit from the moment of their construction and licensing that continues through their long 24-hour a day operations."[254] Granted, internet gaming will not create jobs in the same magnitude as a brick and mortar casino because internet sites have computers performing a lot of work, but it will establish a significant number of customer service, management, and technology jobs. Of course, assuming the Federal Government is licensing the online sites and collecting the revenue, [255] it must find a way to distribute a portion of the proceeds to the states.[256]

Proper federal government regulation might be able to alleviate the state autonomy concerns. Throughout history, states have traditionally regulated gambling within their borders and the federal government has passed statutes only to assist the states in enforcing their gambling regulations.[257] The Wire Act is a great example of this; the Wire Act does not

---

[251] *See* Jeff Simpson, *Experts Promote Legalization of Internet Gambling*, LAS VEGAS REV.J., May 16, 2001, at 3D, available at 2001 WL 9534745.

[252] *See generally* Tratos, *supra* note 44, at 721; Rose & Owens, *supra* note 103; and Lantzer, *supra* note 234: "Not only has Internet gaming in countries with lax regulation grown, but officials in countries such as Australia and Great Britain have legalized Internet gaming establishments in an effort to internalize gaming revenue." The Caribbean islands decided to legalize internet gaming to replace the revenue they have lost as a result of decreased tourism.

[253] *See* Tratos, *supra* note 44, at 754.

[254] *Id.*

[255] *See* Lantzer, *supra* note 234. Lantzer proposes several regulatory schemes including, but not limited to, revising the Federal Wager Tax to distribute tax proceeds to the states on a pro rate basis.

[256] *See* NGIS, *supra* note 210, at 5 and Lantzer, *supra* note 234: "Congress's Power to Regulate Internet Gaming Under the Commerce Clause Congress can clearly regulate Internet gaming under the Commerce Clause. The Commerce Clause allows Congress to regulate commerce with foreign nations or among the several states. Placing bets across state or international lines falls into the category of commerce among the several states or with foreign nations for several reasons."

[257] *See* Lantzer, *supra* note 234: "States traditionally regulate gambling under their police powers. The police power allows states to regulate in the interest of the health, safety, morals, and welfare of citizens. Gambling has historically been regulated by the states under the police power because gambling is considered a vice activity that affects the morality of citizens. The police power gives states the authority to regulate gaming to the point of completely banning all gaming activity within the borders of the state. Federal gaming regulation has been designed and used to assist states in enforcing gambling

determine the legality of the gambling in question; state law does. The Wire Act only provides a federal cause of action for certain violations of state law to make enforcement easier.[258] The federal government can craft its internet gaming regulations in much the same fashion.

In the Safe Port Act, the government did the exact opposite. It made operating an internet gambling site illegal, but left each state the option of legalizing it within the state.[259] It takes far more effort to mobilize a campaign to make something legal than it does to make something illegal. Furthermore, even if a state wanted to make it legal to operate a site in the state, it is unclear if internet poker site operating in state A could accept customers from state B. That, combined with the fact that the government asserts that the Wire and Travel Acts prohibit running a gambling website make it very unlikely that a state will legalize online poker anytime soon.

On the other hand, if the federal government were to legalize internet gaming subject to regulations, each state could decide whether it wants to "opt into" the government regulation scheme.[260] If the state chooses to opt in, the federal government will perform the regulations and share the tax revenue with the state, keeping a portion of the tax itself to cover the costs of the regulations. If the state chooses to opt out, the federal government can either block internet access to gambling websites in specific states or come up with an alternative means of preventing a certain state's citizens from accessing gambling websites.[261]

One might see a contradiction in some of the above statements, namely, a rift between the contentions that under a regulatory scheme if a state opts out it can have the gambling websites blocked, but if a state tries to prohibit internet gaming it will be too hard for the ISP to block a website to just a handful of states. What differentiates these contentions is that under a regulatory scheme, it will not be an ISP that is blocking the website, it will be the website itself that is hindering a player from a forbidden state to gamble on the site. The regulatory schemes are assuming that part and parcel of legalizing internet gaming is mandating that internet gaming operators submit to U.S. jurisdiction.

Moreover, once web gambling is conditionally legalized, internet gambling companies will incorporate in the U.S. either as one of the conditions of their legalization or based on the sheer entrepreneurial spirit of the American people. Many experts agree that "the advantages of setting up Internet gaming sites offshore are outweighed by the opportunity to profit from legalized Internet gaming in the United States and other first-world countries."[262] Other corporations inherently linked to internet gambling, such as e-banks modeled after Neteller and Firepay, will likely follow as well.

Regulation does have its disadvantages, however. It is exceedingly more complicated (excepting the fact that the current prohibition has jurisdictional problems) and requires exceedingly more upfront costs than outright prohibition. Once a prohibition bill is passed, the

---

regulations. The federal government yields to the wishes of the states in determining gambling policy because states are better able to determine the will of the people."

[258]. *Id.* "States determine the legality of placing wagers while the Wire Act assists "prohibitionist states in keeping their citizens free from operators based in foreign jurisdictions." The Wire Act and other federal statutes do not determine the legality of gambling in any particular state or for the nation as a whole. Rather, federal statutes assist states in effectively enforcing their own laws by providing a federal cause of action against violators whom states would otherwise have difficulty prosecuting."

[259]. Safe Port Act H.R. 4954

[260]. *Id.*

[261]. For a discussion of different possible regulatory models *see* Lantzer, *supra* note 234.

[262]. *Id.*

DOJ can immediately begin mandating the compliance ISPs and credit card companies, shutting down the threat with little expenditure of time. Enforcement of a prohibition bill and continued compliance checks is likely to cost the government $10 million annually.[263] Regulation, on the other hand, will require more complicated legislation.[264] It will also require far more governmental monitoring and possibly the creation of a separate sub-regulatory agency.[265] It will also necessitate a tax revenue dispersal scheme which will take time to create. All of this will require much more than $10 million per year.[266] However, legalizing and taxing internet gambling will bring in many millions of dollars more than is needed to regulate it, thus making it a profitable venture for both the federal and state governments.

While prohibition appears to offer a quick fix, regulation can provide revenue to states and help further state sovereignty. It will also help further a long standing American principle—self determination. Most gamblers are not problem gamblers. Most players gamble infrequently for the enjoyment of the experience.[267] Proponents of gambling continue to harp on the idea that these people should not have the government forcing its moral values or social norms upon them.[268] Moreover, as will be discussed in the subsequent section, poker is played for reasons beyond the mere "gamble" of it: the sense of skill involved, the feeling of victory over a group of peers (not the casino), and to make money. The government has recognized being a professional gambler is a lawful profession for tax purposes, yet at the same time this "lawful" profession cannot occur in some states.[269] In the words of gambling author Barry Shulman, people should be able to make "adult personal choices with what to do with their own time and money."[270]

IX) CONCLUSION

With the passage of the internet gambling ban incorporated in the Safe Port Act it seems that the debate raging around prohibiting online gambling versus regulating it has come to a close. However, upon closer examination of the ban, based on the jurisdictional factors discussed above, one can see that the so called "ban" on online gaming is not effective. As long as non-gambling related financial intermediaries remain operational in other countries, this ban will not prohibit online gaming in this country.

---

[263] *See* H.R.4777 109th Cong. (Representative Goodlatte).
[264] *See generally*, DAVID G. SCHWARTZ, CUTTING THE WIRE: GAMBLING PROHIBITION AND THE INTERNET at 193–8, (Univ. Nev. Press, 2005).
[265] *Id.*
[266] *Id.*
[267] For the general proposition, *see, generally*, Roy Cooke, *Stepping Up From Home Poker*, CARDPLAYER MAGAZINE VOL. 19 NO. 8, http://www.cardplayer.com/poker_magazine/archives/showarticle.php?a_id=15412. (last visited May 16, 2006)
[268] *See* PPA, *supra* note 234.
[269] *See, e.g.,* CIT. v. Graettinger, 480 U.S. 23,35–6 (1987): ". . . [W]e conclude that if one's gambling activity is pursued full time, in good faith, and with regularity, to the production of income for a livelihood, and is not a mere hobby, it is a trade or business within the meaning of the statutes with which we are here concerned. Respondent Graettinger satisfied that test in 1978. Constant and large scale effort on his part was made. Skill was required and was applied. He did what he did for a livelihood, though with a less-than-successful result. This was not a hobby or a passing fancy or an occasional bet for amusement."
[270] *See* Barry Shulman, *Congress Scares Me*, THE INSIDE SCOOP, April 16, 2006, http://www.cardplayer.com/poker_news/blog_author/1?page=5

Given the impotence of this ban, the government should not be quick to table the idea of regulating and taxing online gaming especially in light of the fact that there are millions of Americans who enjoy playing the game responsibly. In 1996, the Loyola of Los Angeles Entertainment Law Journal published one of the first articles addressing the legality of the hundreds of casinos that suddenly appeared on the internet. In that article, Seth Gorman and Anthony Loo both recommended and predicted that the U.S. legalize and regulate the internet gambling industry.[271] The authors relied on the fact that 48 out of the 50 states already have some form of legalized gambling and that the tax revenue from these sites could total in the hundreds of millions of dollars each year.[272] In 2002, the Chapman Law review published an article which stated that "the lure of consumer preference and tax revenue" made the legalization of internet gaming inevitable.[273] So far, the U.S. Congress has made no attempts to legalize internet gambling; despite this, the NGISC reports that legalized gambling in the United States has increased exponentially in the past few years.[274]

Even if the government chooses not to revisit its decision to ban online gaming, a strong argument can be made that poker should be differentiated from other forms of gambling. Poker is a game of skill and the law should treat it accordingly.

Most state laws permit wagers to be placed on games of skill without penalty.[275] However, what determines a "game of skill" varies from state to state and often depends on the court's statutory interpretation. An example of a pure game of skill is chess. It is a game of perfect information in which the player with the greater skill at the time of the game will always win.

"The best known games of skill played for money, which are also available online in the United States, are fantasy sports leagues."[276] Proponents of these leagues cite the skills involved in researching, drafting, and trading players; nonetheless, the game involves a "significant element of chance".[277] However, the court has yet to specifically hold that skill predominates chance in fantasy sports leagues so the question of their legality is still up in the air.[278] The most telling point that illustrates that many Americans believe that fantasy sports leagues require skill is that the Safe Port Act contains a specific carve-out for fantasy sports leagues, which exempts them from this law.

No court has specifically stated that poker is a game of skill.[279] No court has specifically stated that poker is a game predominated by chance. However, some dicta sheds light on the issue, indicating that poker is a game that involves elements of both chance and skill. In the Oregon case of *State v. Coats*, the court commented that "poker, when played for money, is a gambling game, but, since it involves a substantial element of skill judgment, it cannot

---

[271] *See* Gorman and Loo, *supra* note 78.
[272] *Id.*
[273] *See* Lantzer, *supra* note 234.
[274] *See* NGIS, *supra* 210 at 1-1,2.
[275] *See, generally,* the individual state laws available at http://www.gambling-law-us.com/State-Laws/
[276] *See* Chuck Humphrey, *Is Poker in the U.S. a Game of Skill?*, http://www.gambling-law-us.com/Articles-Notes/online-poker-skill.htm.
[277] *Id.*
[278] *Id.* citing State v. Hahn, 586 N.W.2d 5 (Wis. 1998): "Whether Fantasy Sports contests are considered gambling is a matter of debate, which revolves around whether skill or chance predominates the contest;" and Davidson, *COMMENT: Internet Gambling: Should Fantasy Sports Leagues Be Prohibited?*, 39 SAN DIEGO L. REV. 201.
[279] *Id.*

reasonably be contended that it is a lottery."[280] Along the same lines, in the Colorado case of *Ginsberg v. Centennial Turf Club*, the court noted that "no one would contend that a game of poker in which money is bet upon the relative value of the cards held by the participants, constitutes a lottery, but it most certainly is a form of gambling."[281]

However, individual state courts have specifically defined what a game of skill is in general. The consensus seems to be that a "game of skill" is a game in which "skill predominates chance" in determining the winner. For example, in *In Re Allen*, the California court defined a game of skill as follows: "It is the character of the game rather than a particular player's skill or lack of it that determines whether the game is one of chance or skill. The test is not whether the game contains an element of chance or an element of skill but which of them is the dominating factor in determining the result of the game."[282] As another example, [283] a Wisconsin statute defines skill in gaming by stating the following: "In this subdivision, 'skill' means, within an opportunity provided for all players fairly to obtain prizes or rewards of merchandise, a player's precision, dexterity or ability to use his or her knowledge which enables him or her to obtain more frequent rewards or prizes than does another less precise, dexterous or knowledgeable player."[284]

Mr. Humphrey contends that poker does not fit the definition of a skill game because for each individual session or over a short period of time (months to a year) skill does not predominate over luck.[285] He does add that in the long-run, skill might predominate over luck.[286] He fails, however, to grasp the complete issue. If a skilled player knows his poker-hand has an 85% chance of beating his opponent's hand, he would like to bet as much as possible. This is an extremely favorable situation for that player. Nonetheless, 15% of the time, this player will lose the hand and his money. Several of these unlucky hands for the skilled player could happen in succession, making him a loser in the game for a day, a month, possibly even up to a year. But, if the skilled player continues to put his money in the pot as an 85% favorite, or just a favorite in general, over time, mathematics dictates that he cannot walk away from the game a loser.[287] There is an abundance of literature discussing how, in the long-run, skill dominates luck at the poker table.[288] In fact, California has already recognized poker as a game of skill, allowing casinos devoted solely to poker while games of chance remain illegal.[289]

To illustrate his point, Mr. Humphrey mentions that few players repeat as "tournament player of the year." However, great tournament players often have consistent results. Looking at the Card Player Magazine player of the year awards, Michael Mizrachi finished in the top 10

---

[280] 74 P.2D 1102,1106 (1938).
[281] 251 P.2D 926, 929 (1952).
[282] 377 P.2D 280 (1961).
[283] WIS. STATS. § 945.01 (3)(b)(3).
[284] These examples, and others from this section, have been taken from an online piece by Humphrey, *supra* note 276.
[285] *See* Humphrey, *supra* note 276.
[286] *Id.*
[287] *See, generally,* DAVID SKYLANSKY, THE THEORY OF POKER, (Two Plus Two Publishing, 1987).
[288] *See* any of the hundreds of poker books or articles, e.g. DOYLE BRUNSON, SUPER SYSTEM, PPA, *supra* note 234, or Smith, infra note 294.
[289] Tie Smith, Poker 101: Its Not Just a Game of Chance, THE DAILY UTAH CHRONICLE, September 1, 2005, http://www.pokerplayersalliance.org/commentary/c090105-2.html: "In fact, many states in this country do not even classify poker as a gambling game; it is classified as a game of skill, like bowling or golf. California, for example, has casinos devoted entirely to the game of poker while casino gambling games classified as games of chance remain illegal."

in his first two years he competed, Men Nguyen finished in the top 15 in 3 of the last 4 years, and Scotty Nguyen finished in the top 20 in each of the last 4 years.[290] Additionally, only 8 players have 8 or more tournament victories at the WSOP.[291] This shows that it takes an elite type of skill to win consistently over time. Furthermore, the point system involved in player of the year awards weighs first place finishes highly and fail to reward a player who consistently finishes in the top 20 in tournament play. In addition, these records do not accurately reflect the tremendous increases in tournament fields in recent years. Moreover, these records do not accurately reflect the best or most consistent players because lots of the world's best player stick strictly to cash games or play only the biggest tournaments each year. Also, because of escalating blind structures, tournament poker has a higher variance than cash games and therefore more luck is involved. No definitive records exists which chronicle the winnings of the world's best cash game players, but there is little doubt that these players exist.[292] Nonetheless, several of the top poker players are consistent winners on the tournament circuit: Victor Ramdin, Daniel Negreanu, Phil Ivey, Doyle Brunson, Barry Greenstein, Scotty Nguyen, and Freddy Deed just to name a handful.[293] Their performances can be likened to the top professionals in tennis or golf tournaments.

Currently, the courts and states are divided as to whether poker should be considered a game of skill; a legal grey area exists here.[294] Poker involves a high amount of skill. Mathematical precision is required to effectively know when to call, bet, and raise. Knowledge of statistics is necessary to know the percentage chance one hand has to beat another. Experience is necessary to help know what to do in given situations and to help determine what an opponent might be holding. Knowledge of psychology is paramount in evaluating the strength of an opponent's hand. Patience and concentration are required to study opponent's betting patterns and tells. Gaming that involves skill is much less likely to cause the negative social spillovers consistently mentioned by anti-gambling activists.[295] As the money in poker is redistributed among players and not given to the house, there is no net loss in wealth to society (except the rake.) A losing poker player is much more likely to either become better or quit playing; this is not the case with the more addictive casino games and slots.[296] The average losing player loses less in poker as compared to table games. (Technically, given that the money

---

[290.] See www.cardplayer.com.
[291.] See http://www.pokerpages.com/pokerinfo/tournamentgallery/wsop/bracelet-winners01.htm.
[292] Brunson *supra* note 293, www.fullcontactpoker.com, neverwinpoker.com
[293.] See id., www.worldpokertur.com, and http://pokerdb.thehendonmob.com/player.php?a=l. (This database enables anyone to look up a professional player's name and see their tournament winnings for the last few decades. You can look up all the players I referred to by going to that link, clicking on "players" and then typing in their respective names. In the poker community, this is the be-all, end-all of player databases.)
[294.] See Charles Humphrey, Esq., *Is Poker in the U.S. a Game of Skill?*, http://www.gambling-law-us.com/Articles-Notes/online-poker-skill.htm. In a footnote concerning the assertion that poker is in a grey area and has been held to be predominately skill-based by "some courts" the author states: "See, e.g., Charnels v. Cent. City Opera House Sass's., 773 P.2d 546, 551 (Colo. 1989) (holding that, in Colorado, poker is an illegal gambling game of chance); see also United States v. Murder, 48 F.3d 564, 569 (1st Cir. 1995) (holding that, in Massachusetts, video poker is a lottery in which chance predominates); *but see* Commonwealth v. Club Caravan, Inc., 571 N.E.2d 405 (Mass. App. Ct. 1991) (holding that, in Massachusetts, video poker games are games of skill); cf. 1993 Colo. Op. AT&T's Gen. No. 93-5 (April 21, 1993) (opining that, in Colorado, poker is a game of skill, but nevertheless illegal under specific statutory language)." Id. at n.41.
[295.] See, generally, PPA, supra 234. Less addictive. Less likely to be played by minors. Less crime associated with it, etc. As money is redistributed amongst players there is no net loss wealth to society.
[296.] Id.

is redistributed amongst the players, the average player is break-even and neither wins nor loses money—but the average loser himself loses less money on average.)[297] Poker is a game of skill and any internet law should reflect that. It is not necessary for the law to legalize poker purely because it is a skill game. But, if skill games are exempt from a gambling prohibition, poker should definitely be included.

Poker is red hot. Tournament poker fields have doubled and tripled over the past few years due to televised poker on ESPN and the Travel channel. Thousands of players have flocked to the newest medium on which to compete, internet poker sites.[298] This paper began its survey of the burgeoning world of internet poker by tracking the history of its legality. After concluding that the government was indeed correct in its assertion that internet poker was prohibited by the Travel and Illegal Gambling Business Acts, it analyzed the recent ban on online gambling passed attached to the Safe Port Act of 2006. However, the U.S. will be unable to enforce these laws against poker operators, who are located in foreign countries unlikely to cooperate with the U.S. in enforcing judgments against them. U.S. players will be able to avoid the intent of this law by sending their money to these sites through Neteller, a financial intermediary incorporated in Canada.

Therefore, the U.S. government should reconsider regulating online poker. Most states already allow some form of card-based gambling. By foregoing regulation, the government is ignoring state sovereignty issues and declining millions of dollars in tax revenue. Moreover, regulation will give the government the ability to monitor online gambling operators and protect social policy by setting age limits. Lastly, legalizing online poker will renew America's longstanding belief in allowing its citizens self-determination.

[297.] *See, generally* Skylansky, *supra* note 292.
[298.] *See, generally,* WO, *supra* note 31.

NETWORK SECURITY ABSTRACT

Julie Machal-Fulks[1]

I) INTRODUCTION

In the four years since California took the lead and enacted SB 1386, many states have followed suit and enacted similar legislation. While many of the provisions are similar, the laws contain varying definitions of personal information. The laws also provide for different types of notification after a security breach. Although this article will include a brief discussion of various state statutes, the differences between the various state laws may be made irrelevant by federal legislation. There are five bills currently under consideration by Congress. It is unclear which, if any, of the pending bills will become the national security breach notification law. What is clear is that if any of the current iterations of the pending legislation is enacted by Congress, businesses will once again have to adapt their business practices because the federal legislation will preempt the current state laws.

II) OVERVIEW OF STATE LEGISLATION

a) Definition of Personal Information

The primary element of the privacy breach notification statutes in the various states is the definition of personal information. Generally, any business that possesses the personal information of a resident of a particular state must notify the resident that his or her personal information has been obtained by an unauthorized individual. Obviously, to determine whether a breach must be reported, it is critical to determine whether information obtained by a hacker qualifies as personal information for purposes of the many different state statutes.

For instance, in California, personal information includes a person's first name or first initial and last name, along with one of the following unencrypted pieces of information:

- social security number;
- driver's license number or state identification number; or
- account number, credit card number, or debit card number, combined with any password, security code, or access code.[2]

The definitions of personal information in Connecticut, Delaware, Florida, Illinois, Louisiana, Minnesota, Montana, Nevada, New Jersey, Rhode Island, Tennessee, Texas, and

---

[1] Julie Machal-Fulks is an expert in IT compliance management and focuses her practice on IT asset management, network security, and privacy. Julie graduated with honors from Texas A&M - Corpus Christi, earning a B.A. in English. She received her law degree from The University of Houston Law Center where she was inducted into the Order of the Barristers. Julie's article, "Privacy, Network Security, and the Law," was recently published in the IT Compliance Journal.

[2] Cal. Civil Code, § 1798.82(e).

Washington are identical to California's definition.[3] Although Indiana's and Ohio's definitions of personal information are identical to California's definition, the notification statutes in these states only apply to state agencies.[4] Private businesses are not required by the Indiana or Ohio statutes to report security breaches.

There are also several states that include more information in the definition of personal information than California. For example, Arkansas' statute contains medical information, as well as the items enumerated in the California definition of personal information.[5] Georgia's and Maine's definitions of personal information include the data components identified in California's statute, as well as account passwords or other personal identification numbers or access codes and any items that, even without the first and last name are sufficient to allow an unauthorized person to attempt identity theft.[6]

North Carolina's statute also expands the California definition to include passport numbers, debit card numbers, digital signatures, any other numbers or information that can be used to access a person's financial resources, biometric data, and fingerprints.[7] North Dakota also includes date of birth, mother's maiden name, identification numbers assigned by employers, and digital signatures.[8] In New York, "personal information" is defined as information concerning a natural person which, because of name, number, personal mark, or other identifier, can be used to identify such natural person. Notification is required when public information is obtained in conjunction with a social security number, driver's license or state identification number, or account number, credit card number, or debit card number, in combination with the security code or password.[9] Businesses that maintain personal information on behalf of clients can significantly reduce the burden of reporting security breaches by encrypting the data. Of the twenty-three states that have enacted security breach notification laws, only five states require notification of a breach of encrypted data (Louisiana, New York, North Carolina, Ohio, and Texas have enacted statutes that require notification even if the personal information data is encrypted).[10]

Businesses that expect to incorporate provisions into their customer contracts waiving the statutory notification provisions should beware. Most privacy breach notification statutes include provisions that any attempt to waive the statutory obligations is void because it is against public policy. For more information regarding the other components of the state statutes, please refer to Figure 1.

Figure 1

---

[3] See Conn. Gen. Stat. Ann. § 36a-701b(a) (West 2006); Del. Code Ann. tit. 6 § 12B-101 (2006); Fla. Stat. Ann. § 817.5681(d)(5) (West 2006); 815 Ill. Comp. Stat. § 530/5 (West 2006); La. Rev. Stat. Ann. § 51:3073(4) (West 2006); Me. Rev. Stat. Ann. tit. 10, § 1347(6) (2006); Minn. Stat. Ann. § 325E.61(e) (West 2006); Mont. Code Ann. § 30-14-1704(4)(b) (2005); Nev. Rev. Stat. Ann. § 603A.040 (West 2005); N.J. Stat. Ann. § 56:8-161 (West 2006); 73 Pa. Stat. Ann. § 2302 (West 2006); R.I. Gen. Laws § 11-49.2-5(c) (West 2006); Tenn. Code Ann. § 47-18-2107(a)(3) (West 2006); Tex. Bus. & Com. Code Ann. §§ 48.002, 48.103 (Vernon 2006); Wash. Rev. Code Ann. § 19.255.010(5) (West 2006).
[4] See Ind. Code Ann. § 4-1-11-3 (West 2006); Ohio Rev. Code Ann. § 1349.19(A)(7) (West 2006).
[5] Ark. Code Ann. 4-110-103 (West 2006).
[6] Ga. Code Ann. § 10-1-911(5) (West 2006); Me. Rev. Stat. Ann. tit. 10, § 1347(6) (West 2006).
[7] N.C. Gen. Stat. Ann. §§ 75-61(10), 14-113.20(b) (West 2006).
[8] N.D. Cent. Code § 51-30-01(2)(a) (West 2005).
[9] N.Y. Gen. Bus. Law § 899-aa(1)(a)-(b) (McKinney 2006).
[10] See La. Rev. Stat. Ann. § 51:3073 (West 2006); N.Y. Gen. Bus. Law § 899-aa (McKinney 2006); N.C. Gen. Stat. Ann. §§ §§ 75-61(10), 14-113.20(b) (West 2006); Ohio Rev. Code Ann. § 1349.19 (West 2006); Tex. Bus. & Com. Code Ann. §§ 48.002, 48.103 (Vernon 2006).

State Security Breach Notification Laws [11]

State	Time To Notify Consumers of a Breach of Personal Information	Civil Penalties for failure to promptly notify customers of breach	Private Right of Action	Exemption for Encrypted Personal Info	Exemption for Criminal Investigations or Information publicly available from government entities	Exemption for Immaterial Breaches (typically defined as no reasonable likelihood of harm)
Arizona	Most expedient time possible, without unreasonable delay	X		X	X	
Arkansas	Most expedient time possible, without unreasonable delay	X		X	X	X
California	Most expedient time possible, without unreasonable delay		X	X	X	
Colorado	Most expedient time possible, without unreasonable delay	X		X	X	X
Connecticut	Immediately			X	X	X
Delaware	Immediately, in the Most expedient time possible, without unreasonable delay	X	X	X	X	
Florida	Without unreasonable delay	X		X	X	
Georgia	Most expedient time possible, without unreasonable delay			X	X	
Illinois	Most expedient time possible, without unreasonable delay		X	X	X	
Hawaii	Without unreasonable delay	X	X	X	X	
Idaho	Most expedient time possible, without unreasonable delay	X		X	X	X
Indiana	Without unreasonable delay			X	X	
Kansas	Most expedient time possible, without unreasonable delay	X		X	X	X

---

[11] The Arizona law becomes effective on December 31, 2006 and the Kansas and Utah laws become effective on January 1, 2007.

State	Timing	Col1	Col2	Col3	Col4	Col5
Louisiana	Most expedient time possible, without unreasonable delay		X		X	X
Maine	As expediently as possible, without unreasonable delay	X		X	X	
Minnesota	Most expedient time possible, without unreasonable delay	X		X	X	
Montana	Without unreasonable delay	X		X	X	
Nebraska	Without unreasonable delay	X		X	X	X
Nevada	As soon as possible, without unreasonable delay	X	X[12]	X	X	
New Hampshire	As soon as possible.	X	X	X	X	X
New Jersey	Most expedient time possible, without unreasonable delay			X	X	X
New York	Most expedient time possible, without unreasonable delay	X				
North Carolina	Without unreasonable delay	X	X		X	X
North Dakota	Most expedient time possible, without unreasonable delay			X	X	
Ohio	Most expedient time possible, but not later than 45 days	X			X	X
Oklahoma	Most expedient time possible, without unreasonable delay			X	X	
Pennsylvania	Without Unreasonable delay	X		X	X	
Rhode Island	Most expedient time possible, without unreasonable delay	X	X	X	X	X
Tennessee	Most expedient time possible, without unreasonable delay		X	X	X	
Texas	As quickly as	X			X	

---

[12] The private cause of action is assigned to the data collector whose information was breached against the party responsible for the breach.

State	Timing					
Utah	Most expedient time possible, without unreasonable delay	X		X	X	X
Vermont	Most expedient time possible, without unreasonable delay	X		X	X	X
Washington	Most expedient time possible, without unreasonable delay		X	X	X	X
Wisconsin	Within a reasonable time, not to exceed 45 days				X	

b) Notification After Personal Information Has Been Breached.

Most of the jurisdictions also followed California's lead when describing the type of notice required for security breaches. The vast majority of states allow written notice or electronic notice provided in accordance with 15 U.S.C. § 7001. If the person or business providing the notice demonstrates that the number of affected persons exceeds 500,000 or that the cost of notice would exceed $250,000, then notice may be provided via electronic mail, via posting on the person or business' website, or via publication in major statewide media.

Five states allow telephone notification in addition to the notice described above. Delaware, Maine, Montana, North Carolina, and Pennsylvania allow notification via telephone, with varying degrees of restrictions. For instance, Maine requires those providing telephonic notice to maintain a log, Pennsylvania only allows telephonic notice if the customer can reasonably be expected to receive the notice and it is given in a clear, conspicuous manner, and North Carolina requires that contact be made directly with the affected person.[13]

III) PENDING FEDERAL LEGISLATION

a) The Notification of Risk to Personal Data Act.

The proposed Notification of Risk to Personal Data Act (NRPDA) was introduced in the Senate on June 28, 2005 by Senator Jefferson Sessions [R-AL].[14] The bill, which has been approved in committee and is not before the entire Senate, is the legislation currently pending in the Senate that is most like the California statute. The bill would preempt all the state notification laws and would require notification if there is a breach of sensitive personal information that results in a significant risk of identity theft to any individual. Notification must be made as expediently as possible and without unreasonable delay.

The definition of sensitive personal information differs slightly from that of the states. For purposes of the NRPDA, sensitive personal information includes an individual's first and last name, the individual's address or telephone number, and the social security number, driver's license or state identification number, financial account number, credit or debit card number and any required security or access code or password. Like many state laws, the

---

[13] *See* Del. Code Ann. tit. 6 § 12B-101 (2006); Me. Rev. Stat. Ann. tit. 10, § 1347(6) (2006); Mont. Code Ann. § 30-14-1704(4)(b) (2005); N.C. Gen. Stat. Ann. §§ 75-61(10), 14-113.20(b) (West 2006); 73 Pa. Stat. Ann. § 2302 (West 2006).

[14] Notification of Risk to Personal Data Act, S. 1326, 109th Cong. (2005).

NRPDA excludes publicly available information and encrypted information from the definition of sensitive personal information. Similarly, notification is not required if notification would impede a civil or criminal investigation.

Under this legislation, notice could be given in writing, by telephone, e-mail, or in certain circumstances, by posting on the Internet or notifying the media. Before sending notice to more than 1,000 individuals, those required to give notice must also notify consumer credit reporting agencies as to the number of individuals impacted and the type of notice that will be given to individuals.

The most significant differences between the state security breach laws and the NRPDA are the enforcement provisions. Violations of the NRPDA would be enforced by the "functional regulator." The functional regulator is the appropriate government entity based on the type of agency or business that violated the provisions of the NRPDA. For instance, if an insurance agency violated the NRPDA, the state insurance authority would enforce the provisions; if an air carrier failed to comply with the provisions, the Secretary of Transportation would be the functional regulator. State Attorneys General could also bring actions in federal court for violations of the NRPDA.[15]

b) The Identity Theft Protection Act

The proposed Identity Theft Protection Act (ITPA) is currently pending in the Senate.[16] It was introduced on July 14, 2005 by Senator Gordon Smith [R-OR] and is currently scheduled for debate. The ITPA expressly preempts all state and local laws governing security breach notification.[17] The current version of the bill provides that a covered entity has to notify the Federal Trade Commission (FTC), possibly all credit reporting agencies, and possibly consumers of breaches in security. A Covered entity is defined as "a sole proprietorship, partnership, corporation, trust, estate, cooperative, association, or other commercial entity, and any charitable, educational, or nonprofit organization that acquires, maintains, or utilizes sensitive personal information."[18]

The sensitive personal information definition in the ITPA is similar, but not identical to, California's definition. Sensitive personal information is an individual's name, address, or telephone number combined with one or more of the following pieces of information:

- social security or other taxpayer number;
- financial account number, credit card number, or debit card number, combined with the required security code, access code, or password; or
- state driver's license identification number or state resident identification number.[19]

Unlike the state laws, covered entities would be required to notify various agencies based on the number of individuals affected by the breach. If 1,000 or more individuals are affected by the breach, the covered agency must report the breach to the FTC, as well as all of the consumer credit reporting agencies.[20] If fewer than 1,000 individuals are impacted and if the covered entity determines that the breach does not create a reasonable risk of identity theft, the covered entity must report the breach to the FTC but not to the consumer reporting agencies.[21]

---

[15] See S. 1326 § 3(c)(1). The proposed legislation prohibits private causes of action. See id. § 3(c)(2).
[16] Identity Theft Protection Act, S. 1408, 109th Cong. (2005).
[17] See id. § 7.
[18] See id. § 10(4).
[19] See id. § 10(9).
[20] See id. § 3(a).
[21] See id. § 3(b).

Regardless of the number of persons affected, covered entities would also be required to notify consumers of the breach when there is a reasonable risk of identity theft. Notification pursuant to this provision must take place in the most expedient manner practicable, but not later than 45 days after the date the breach was discovered by the covered entity.[22]

To determine whether there is a reasonable risk of identity theft, covered entities must consider a number of factors. The proposed legislation requires covered entities to evaluate whether the data contains sensitive personal information usable by an unauthorized third party and whether the data is in the possession and control of an unauthorized party likely to commit identity theft. The notice provisions related to consumers are very similar to the state provisions – written or electronic notice and substitute notice under certain circumstances.[23]

Like the majority of state laws, under the ITPA, covered entities would not have to notify consumers of a breach when notice would materially impede a civil or criminal investigation or when notification would threaten national security.[24] The ITPA would be enforced by the FTC, as well as other relevant federal agencies (e.g., the Securities and Exchange Commission would have power to enforce the ITPA with respect to broker/dealers). Although civil penalties are authorized under the ITPA, there would be no private right of action.[25]

c) The Personal Data Privacy and Security Act

The Personal Data Privacy and Security Act (PDPSA) is also currently pending in the Senate. It was introduced on September 29, 2005 by Senators Arlen Specter [R-PA], Russell Feingold [D-WI], Dianne Feinstein [D-CA], and Patrick Leahy [D-VT].[26] The bill has been sent by the committee to be considered by the entire Senate. The PDPSA does not apply to financial institutions, entities covered by HIPAA, or any business that qualifies for exemption under the Safe Harbor provision.[27] The Safe Harbor provision exempts businesses that provide protection equal to industry standards, as identified by the FTC.[28]

All other agencies or business entities engaged in interstate commerce that use access, transmit, store, dispose of, or collect sensitive personally identifiable information, would be required to notify any resident of the United States whose information has been, or is reasonably believed to have been accessed or acquired.[29] This notification must be provided without unreasonable delay. Sensitive personally identifiable information is defined as an individual's first name or first initial and last name, and:

- a non-truncated social security number, driver's
- license number, passport number, or alien
- registration number;
- two of the following;
    - home address or telephone number;
    - mother's maiden name;
    - complete birth day;

---

[22] See id. § 3(e).
[23] See id. § 3(d).
[24] See id. § 3(e)(2).
[25] See id. § 5(f).
[26] Personal Data Privacy and Security Act, S. 1789, 109th Cong. (2005).
[27] See id. Title 3, § 301(c).
[28] See id. § 301(d).
[29] See id. § 321.

- fingerprint, voiceprint, retina or iris image, or any other unique physical representation; or
- a unique account identifier, electronic identification number, user name, or routing code, in combination with any associated security code, access code, or password.[30]

Additionally, sensitive personally identifiable information includes a financial account number, credit card number, or debit card number, "in combination with any security code, access code, or password that is required for an individual to obtain money, goods, services, or any other thing of value."[31]

The notification provisions would not apply to an agency, if the agency certifies in writing that notification may hinder an investigation or cause damage to national security. Businesses would not have to follow the notification provisions if a risk assessment indicates that there is no significant risk of harm to the individuals and the business notifies the Secret Service of the results of the risk assessment without unreasonable delay but not later than 45 days after the breach. Businesses would also be required to notify the Secret Service of their intent to invoke the risk-assessment exemption. The Secret Service would then have 10 days to compel the business to provide notice.

Businesses that are required to disclose security breaches under the PDPSA would be required to provide individual notice and media notice. The individual notice requirements would be satisfied by providing written notice, telephone notice to the individual personally, or e-mail notice if the individual consented to receive such notice. Additionally, if more than 1,000 individuals are involved, the agency or business must notify all consumer credit reporting agencies.

Additionally, the agency or business must give notice of the security breach to the Secret Service if the number of individuals affected exceeds 10,000, if the database accessed contains sensitive personally identifiable information of more than 1,000,000 individuals, if the breached database is owned by the federal government, or if the sensitive personally identifiable information is that of federal government employees or contractors.

Like the ITPA, the PSPDA would completely preempt state laws regarding security breach notifications. The proposed legislation expressly prohibits private causes of action for injuries related to security breaches, but it does provide for civil penalties in actions instituted by the Attorney General.

d) The Financial Data Protection Act

The proposed Financial Data Protection Act (FDPA) was introduced on October 6, 2005 by Representative Steven LaTourette [R-OH] and 14 co-sponsors.[32] This bill has not made it out of the House committee. Most bills do not progress from committee to the entire House. If passed, this legislation would also completely preempt all state security breach notification laws.

The FDPA would amend the Fair Credit Reporting Act. The FDPA requires consumer reporters to investigate potential breaches of sensitive personal information. Consumer reporter is defined as "any consumer reporting agency or financial institution, or any person which, for monetary fees, dues, on a cooperative nonprofit basis, or otherwise regularly engages in whole or in part in the practice of assembling or evaluating consumer reports, consumer credit information, or other information on consumers." Sensitive financial personal

---

[30] See id. § 1(11).
[31] Id.
[32] Financial Data Protection Act, H.R. 3997, 109th Cong. (2005).

information includes a financial account number combined with an access, security, or biometric code or other password or personal identification information. It also includes the first and last name, address or telephone number, and any either a social security number, driver's license or identification number, or taxpayer identification number.

If the breach may result in substantial harm or inconvenience to any consumer to whom the information relates, the consumer reporter must promptly notify:

- the Secret Service;
- the appropriate regulatory agency;
- any entity that owns or is obligated on a financial account that may be subject to unauthorized transactions as a result of the breach;
- if the breach involves 1,000 or more consumers, each nationwide consumer reporting agency ; and
- any appropriate critical third party.[33]

Consumer reporters must also provide notice to consumers if there is a breach that results in a reasonable probability that personal information may be misused. This notice must be made without unreasonable delay. If requested, the consumer reporter must make free credit monitoring services available to consumers for six months. Consumer reporters may delay notice if notice would impede a current civil or criminal investigation. The functional regulatory agencies would be responsible for enforcement of the FDPA.

e) The Data Accountability and Trust Act

The proposed Data Accountability and Trust Act (DATA) was introduced on October 26, 2005 by Representative Clifford Stearns [R-FL] and 8 co-sponsors.[34] It also has not progressed from the committee and would preempt state law.

The DATA would require any person engaged in interstate commerce to (1) report a breach of security to every individual whose personal information was acquired by an unauthorized source, (2) to notify the FTC, (3) to place a conspicuous notice on the Internet website of the person, and (4) if the breach involves financial account information, to notify the financial institution that issued the account.[35] Notification must be made as promptly as possible and without unreasonable delay. Persons could notify individuals of the breach in writing or via electronic mail, and the proposed law would also allow substitute notification if certain criteria were met.

For purposes of the DATA, personal information includes an individual's first and last name and any one of the following:

- social security number;
- driver's license number or other state identification number; or
- financial account number, credit card number, debit card number, and any required security code, access code, or password.

This proposed legislation would require each person providing notification to individuals to also provide a free copy of the individuals' credit report from at least one major credit reporting agency.

---

[33] See *id.* § 630(c).
[34] Data Accountability and Trust Act, H.R. 4127, 190th Cong. (2005).
[35] See *id.* § 3(a).

The FTC would enforce violations of the DATA. Although the bill would preempt state notification laws, it specifically excludes from preemption actions based on state trespass, contract, and tort laws as well as other state laws relating to acts of fraud.[36] In other words, if this legislation were enacted, individuals might be able to seek redress under state law for injuries resulting from unauthorized disclosure of their personal information.

IV) THE NEW STANDARD OF CARE – HOW TO AVOID LIABILITY

Security breaches can be costly. In the past several months, the FTC has investigated and sanctioned several companies for lapses in security involving customer information. For instance, Superior Mortgage Company was accused of misrepresentation by the FTC because although it claimed its data was encrypted, the information was decrypted before it was transmitted via electronic mail to its headquarters.[37] Superior Mortgage agreed to refrain from making misrepresentations and submitted to FTC monitoring for 10 years. DSW was sanctioned for storing unencrypted files that were easily accessed using a commonly known user name and password. DSW agreed to implement comprehensive security measures and submit to FTC compliance monitoring for 20 years.[38] ChoicePoint agreed to pay the $15 million in fines and restitution and allow 20 years of monitoring after it provided sensitive personal information to subscribers who did not have a permissible purpose.[39]

Based on the current state laws it is clear that businesses should, at the very least, ensure that all names, addresses, account numbers, and other personal information of consumers is encrypted. This will minimize the risk that the business will have to notify consumers or law enforcement agencies should a breach occur. Until federal legislation is enacted, businesses must also be aware of the various state law statutes governing the protection of data to determine whether they meet the standards. It may be useful to regularly consult with your attorneys regarding the requirements in the relevant jurisdictions. Ensuring that you comply with the statutes governing the storage of information will also decrease the risk of liability.

Although many state laws do not allow private causes of action based on the security breach laws, other claims based on breach of contract, misrepresentation, or negligence may not be precluded. For instance consumers in many states can file lawsuits against companies, whose security was breached, claiming that the companies negligently stored or protected the information. In addition to being diligent about data protection, companies should also review their contracts and sales materials to ensure that in addition to meeting all the statutory requirements, they are also fulfilling all of their promises to their customers.

V) CONCLUSION

Until federal legislation creates a uniform standard and possibly prohibits private causes of action for security breaches or notifications thereof, businesses must constantly familiarize themselves with the ever-evolving notification requirements for each state in which they do business. With diligent efforts, companies can reduce the possibility of liability for breaches in security.

---

[36] See *id.* § 6(c).
[37] *In the Matter of Superior Mortgage Corporation*, FTC Docket No. C-4153 (Dec. 14, 2005).
[38] *In the Matter of DSW, Inc.*, FTC Docket No. C-4157 (March 7, 2006).
[39] *United States v. ChoicePoint*, No. 1:06-CV-0198 (N.D. Geor. filed Jan. 30, 2006).

www.ingramcontent.com/pod-product-compliance
Lightning Source LLC
Chambersburg PA
CBHW070300220526
45465CB00004B/1675